The IQ Workout Series

MORE IQ TESTING

250 new ways to release your IQ potential

Philip Carter and Ken Russell

JOHN WILEY & SONS, LTD

Published 2002 by John Wiley & Sons Ltd,
Baffins Lane, Chichester,
West Sussex PO19 1UD, England

National   01243 779777
International (+44) 1243 779777
e-mail (for orders and customer service enquiries):
cs-books@wiley.co.uk
Visit our Home Page on http://www.wiley.co.uk
or http://www.wiley.com

Other Wiley Editorial Offices

John Wiley & Sons, Inc., 605 Third Avenue,
New York, NY 10158-0012, USA

WILEY-VCH Verlag GmbH, Pappelallee 3,
D-69469 Weinheim, Germany

John Wiley & Sons Australia Ltd, 33 Park Road, Milton,
Queensland 4064, Australia

John Wiley & Sons (Asia) Pte Ltd, 2 Clementi Loop #02-01,
Jin Xing Distripark, Singapore 129809

John Wiley & Sons (Canada) Ltd, 22 Worcester Road,
Rexdale, Ontario M9W 1L1, Canada

British Library Cataloguing in Publication Data

A catalogue record for this book is available from the British Library

ISBN 0-470-84717-4

Typeset in 11/14 pt Garamond Book by Dorwyn Ltd, Rowlands Castle, Hants.
Printed and bound in Great Britain by Biddles Ltd, Guildford and King's Lynn.

This book is printed on acid-free paper responsibly manufactured from sustainable forestry, in which at least two trees are planted for each one used for paper production.

Contents

Introduction

Intelligence is the capacity to learn or understand. Although intelligence is possessed by all people, it varies in amount for each person, and remains the same throughout life from approximately 18 years of age.

In psychology, intelligence is defined as the capacity to acquire knowledge or understanding, and to use it in novel situations.

What is IQ?

IQ is the abbreviation for intelligence quotient.

Intelligence quotient (IQ) is an age-related measure of intelligence and is defined as 100 times mental age. The word 'quotient' means the result of dividing one quantity by another, and intelligence can be defined as mental ability and quickness of mind.

What is an IQ test?

IQ tests are part of what is generally referred to as 'psychological testing'. Such test content may be addressed to almost any aspect of our intellectual or emotional make-up, including personality, attitude, intelligence or emotion.

An intelligence test (IQ test) is, by definition, any test that purports to measure intelligence. Generally such tests consist of a series of tasks, each of which has been standardized with a large representative population of individuals. Such a procedure establishes the average IQ as 100.

When measuring the IQ of a child, that child is given an intelligence test that has already been given to thousands of other children, so that an average score has been established for each age group. Thus, a child who at 8 years of age obtained a result expected of a 10-year-old would score an IQ of 125, that figure being mental age divided by chronological age $\times$ 100, or 10/8 $\times$ 100. On the other hand, a child of 10 years of age who obtained a result expected of an 8-year-old would score an IQ of 80, or 8/10 $\times$ 100.

Because mental age remains constant from the age of 18 this method of calculation does not apply to adults. Adults have, instead, to be judged on a standardized IQ test whose average score is 100, and the results graded above and below this score according to known scores.

Culture-fair IQ testing

As mastery of words is seen by many as the true measure of intelligence, vocabulary tests have been widely used in intelligence testing. Today, however, there is also a swing towards diagrammatic tests where logic is more important than word knowledge. Advocates of such non-verbal tests argue that diagrammatic tests examine raw intelligence without the influence of prior knowledge.

Such tests are referred to as culture-fair tests, or culture-free tests, and are designed to be free of any particular cultural bias so that no advantage is derived by individuals of one culture relative to those of another. In other words, they eliminate language factors or other skills that may be closely tied to another culture.

How to use this book

The tests in this book are culture-fair and rely mainly on diagrammatical representation. However, numerical skill is also tested as numbers are international and, in the same way as diagrammatic representation, they test powers of logic, and your ability to deal with problems in a structured and analytical way.

The questions in this book are also designed to make you think laterally and creatively, and the developing of such skills can also prove invaluable in dealing with the many real-life problems that you may encounter. They will also provide valuable practice for readers who may have to take an IQ test in the future.

Because the tests have been specially compiled for this book they have not been standardized; therefore, an actual IQ rating cannot be provided. We do, however, provide a guide to assessing your performance on each of the separate tests.

The tests in the book are divided into two main sections. In Part one we provide six separate tests, each of which test a particular type of discipline. A time limit of **60 minutes** is allowed for each of these six tests.

In Part two we provide seven complete IQ tests, which bring together each of these disciplines. A time limit of **80 minutes** is allowed for each of these seven tests.

We would recommend that you attempt the six tests in Part one first as this will then provide practice on the type of questions you are likely to encounter in Part two, which should then enhance your performance on these seven complete tests.

On all of the tests you have limited time, and this time limit should be strictly adhered to, otherwise your score will be invalidated. It is, therefore, important that you do not spend too much time on any one question; if in doubt leave it and return to it using the time remaining. If you do not know an answer, it may be well worth while having an intuitive guess as this may well prove to be correct.

Answers are provided for all questions together with detailed explanations.

Part one

Visual analogy test

1

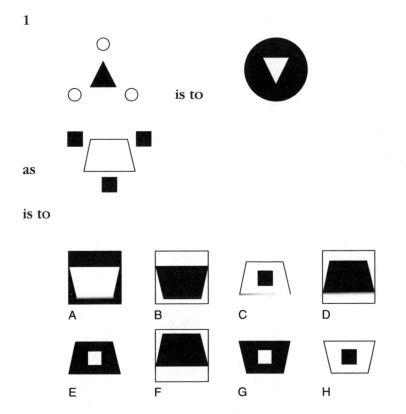

2

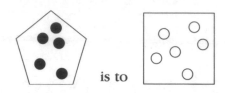

as

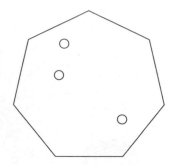

is to

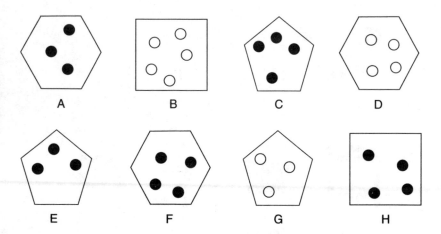

3

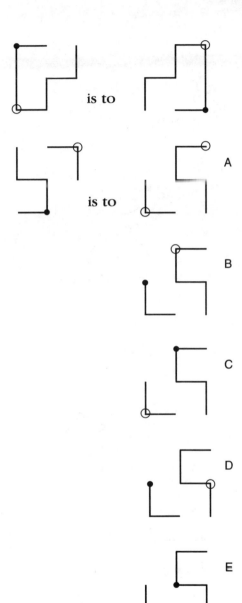

is to

as

is to

A

B

C

D

E

4

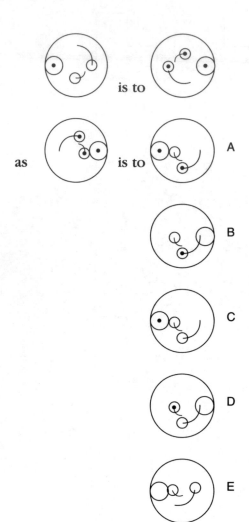

5

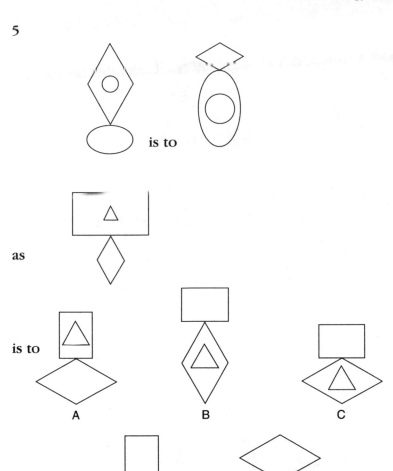

6

is to

as

is to

A   B   C

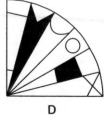 

D   E

7

as

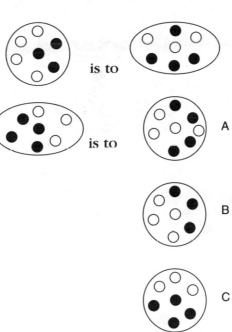

8

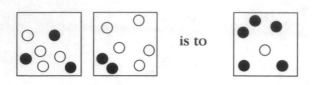

as

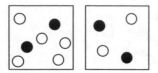

is to

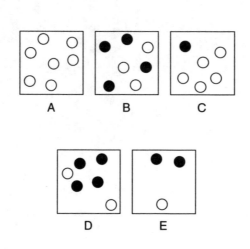

9

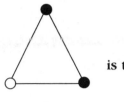

is to

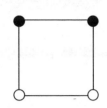

as

is to

 A

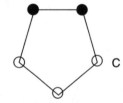 B

C

 D

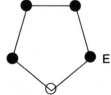 E

10

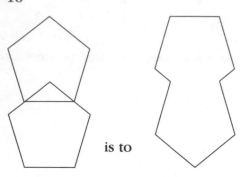

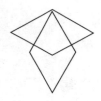 is to

as

is to

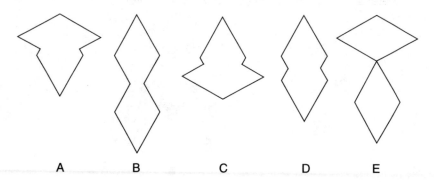

A   B   C   D   E

11

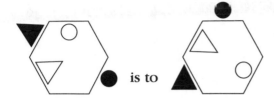

as

is to

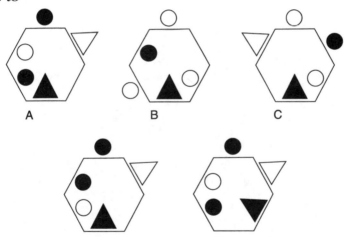

12

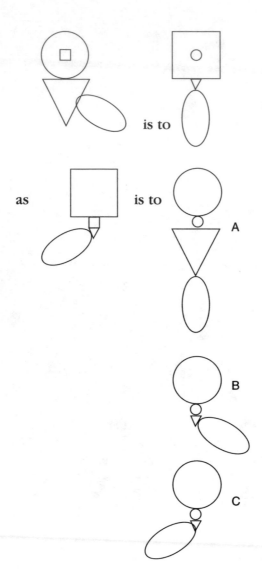

13

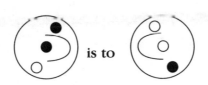

as

A

B

C

D

14

is to   as

is to

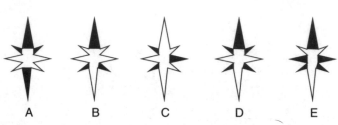

A   B   C   D   E

15

is to

as   is to

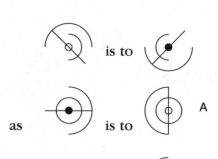

A

B

C

D

E

Visual odd one out test

1 Which is the odd one out?

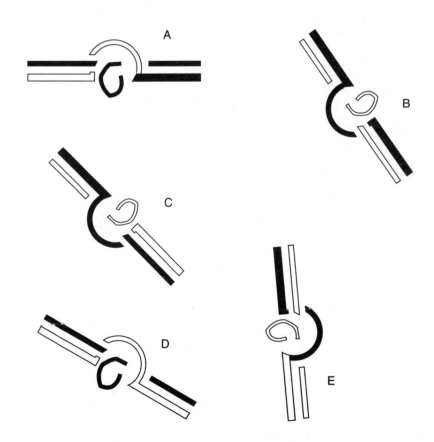

2   Which is the odd one out?

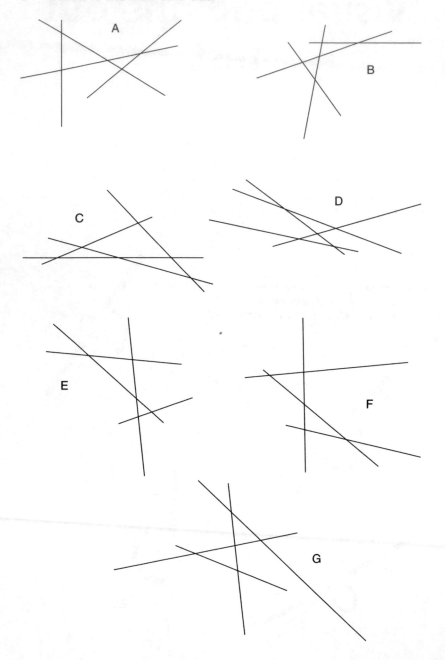

3   Which is the odd one out?

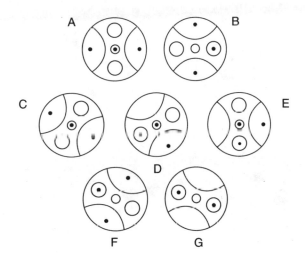

4   Which is the odd one out?

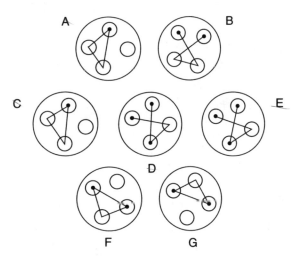

5   Which is the odd one out?

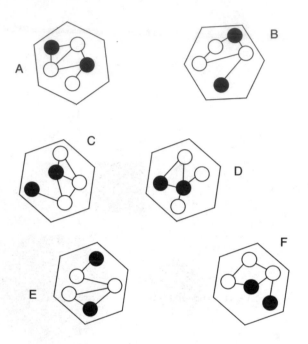

6   Which is the odd one out?

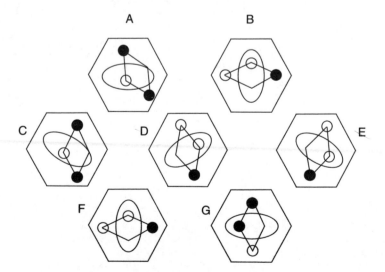

7   Which is the odd one out?

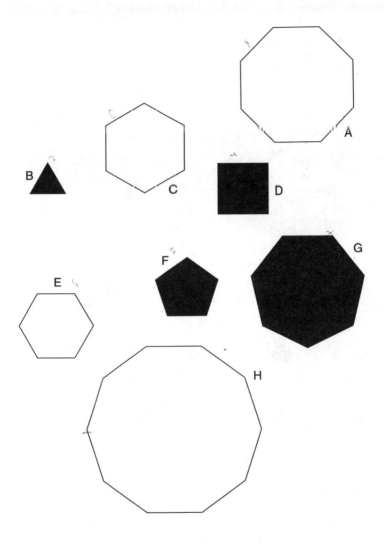

8   Which is the odd one out?

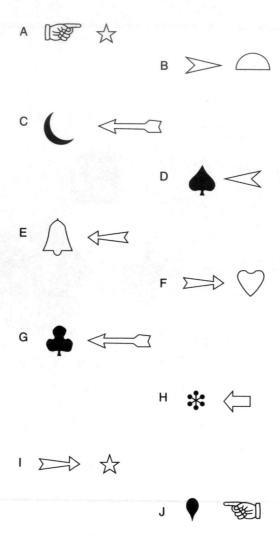

9   Which is the odd one out?

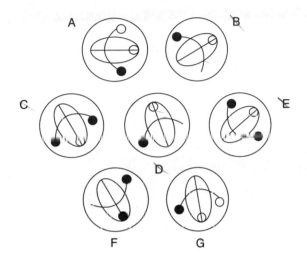

10   Which is the odd one out?

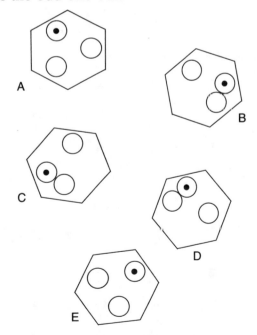

11   Which is the odd one out?

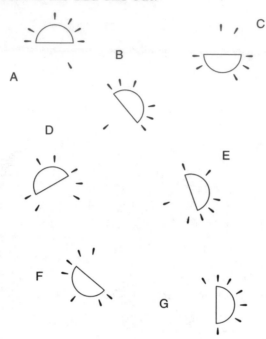

12   Which is the odd one out?

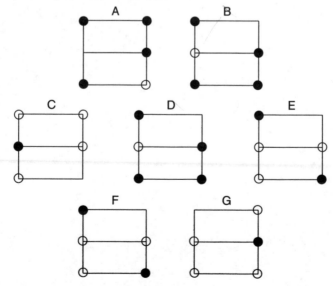

13   Which is the odd one out?

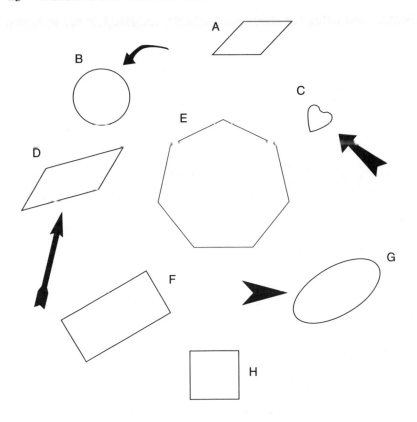

14   Which is the odd one out?

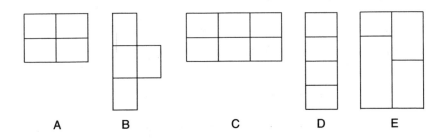

A   B   C   D   E

15   Which is the odd one out?

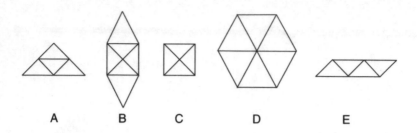

A   B   C   D   E

Lateral thinking test

1   What number should replace the question mark?

7	3
2	5

9	4
8	?

2	1
6	2

2

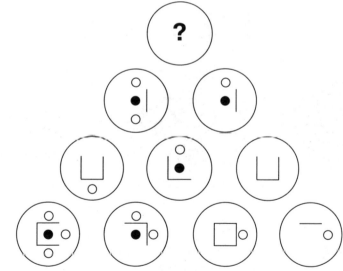

Which circle should replace the question mark?

A   B   C   D

3 What number should replace the question mark?

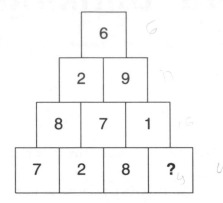

4 Which letter should come next?

FHEXT ?

Choose from:

YKZLI

5 The supervisor said to the carpenter, 'The locks on three of the first seven doors are faulty.'
The carpenter looked at door number 7 first. Why didn't he look at number 1 first?

| 1 | 2 | 3 | 4 | 5 | 6 | 7 | 8 |

| 9 | 10 | 11 | 12 | 13 | 14 | 15 | 16 |

6   Which letter comes next?

   H   N   Y   F   K

Choose from:

   M   T   Z   L

7   Which circle should replace the question mark?

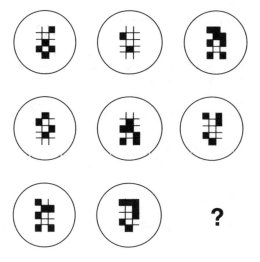

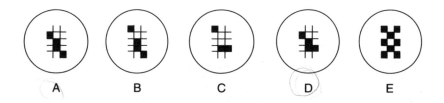

A   B   C   D   E

8

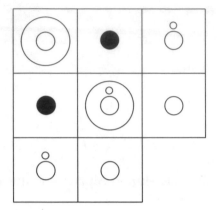

Which is the missing square?

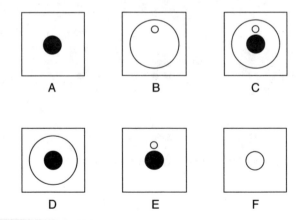

9

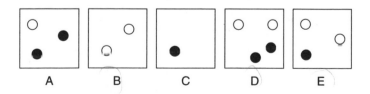

Which square should replace the question mark?

A   B   C   D   E

10

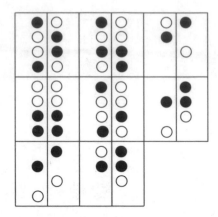

Which is the missing square?

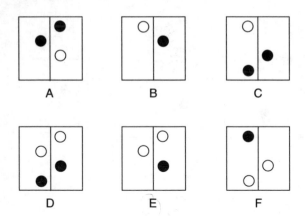

11   Which letter should replace the question mark?

O   D   Q   P   B   ?

Is it:

S   G   R   U   C   or   J   ?

12

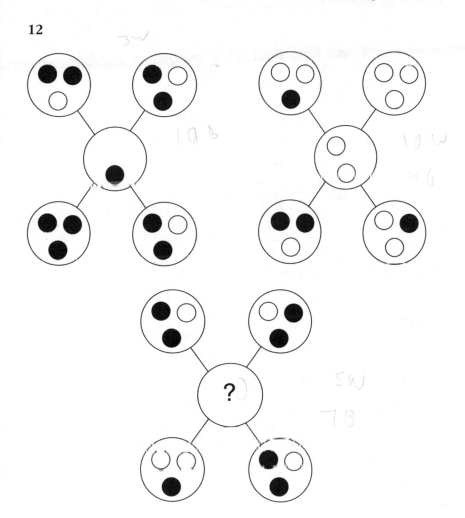

Which circle should replace the question mark?

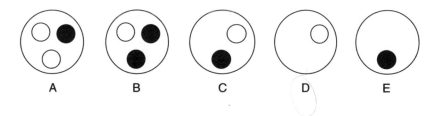

A   B   C   D   E

13 In my fish tank I have 25 zebra fish. The male fish have
   15 stripes each and the female fish have 45 stripes each.
   If I take out two-thirds of the female fish, how many
   stripes in total are left in the tank?

14 What number should replace the question mark?

		2			3	2
	3		3	4	4	
2		3			3	
3			2			2
3	4		3		3	
3		3	3		3	2
?				2		

15 I take a certain journey and, due to heavy traffic, travel
   the first half of the complete distance at a speed of just
   10 m.p.h. How fast would I have to travel over the
   second half of the journey to bring my average speed
   for the whole journey to 20 m.p.h.?

Which letter comes next test

A	B	C	D	E	
F	G	H	I	J	
K	L	M	N	O	
P	Q	R	S	T	
U	V	W	X	Y	Z

1　Which letter comes two below the letter immediately to the right of the letter H?

2　Which letter comes three to the left of the letter that comes two below the letter two to the right of the letter H?

3　Which letter comes two above the letter immediately to the left of the letter immediately above the letter two to the left of the letter X?

4   Which letter comes two to the right of the letter that comes immediately below the letter immediately to the left of the letter two below the letter J?

5   Which letter is two to the right of the letter immediately below the letter that comes two to the left of the letter immediately below the letter D?

6   Which letter is immediately above the letter that is two to the right of the letter that comes midway between the letters J and F?

7   Which letter is immediately to the left of the letter that comes midway between the letter immediately below the letter T and the letter immediately above the letter R?

8   Which letter is three to the left of the letter that is immediately below the letter that is immediately to the left of the letter that is three letters below the letter E?

9   Which letter is two letters below the letter that is two to the left of the letter that is two letters above the letter that is three letters to the right of the letter K?

10   Which letter is two letters below the letter that is immediately below the letter that is three letters to the right of the letter that is two letters above the letter immediately above the letter that is four letters to the left of the letter Z?

11   Which letter is two letters above the letter that is
     immediately to the right of the letter that is immediately
     below the letter that lies midway between the letters A
     and Y?

12   Which letter is immediately below the letter that lies
     midway between the letter that is two letters above the
     letter immediately to the left of the letter L and the
     letter that is immediately above the letter that is
     immediately above the letter immediately to the right of
     the letter N?

13   Which letter is two letters above the letter that is three
     letters to the left of the letter that is immediately to the
     right of the letter that is two letters above the letter that
     is immediately to the left of the letter two letters to the
     left of the letter Z?

14   Which letter is immediately above the letter that is two
     to the right of the letter immediately below the letter
     that comes midway between the letter two letters to the
     left of the letter D and the letter that comes
     immediately to the right of the letter that comes two
     letters below the letter K?

15   Which letter comes midway between the letter that
     comes two letters above the letter that comes
     immediately above the letter two letters to the left of
     the letter R and the letter that comes three letters below
     the letter that is immediately to the right of the letter
     that comes two letters above the letter immediately to
     the left of the letter T?

Visual sequence test

1

Complete the next circle in the above sequence.

2

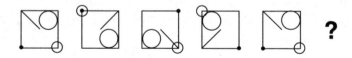 **?**

What comes next?

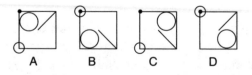

3

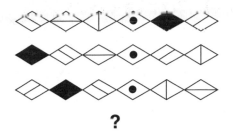

?

What comes next?

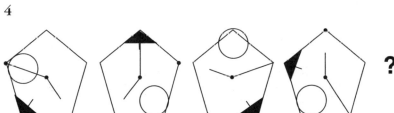

4

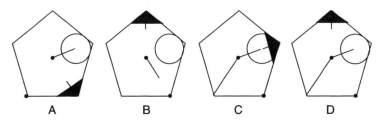

?

What comes next?

5

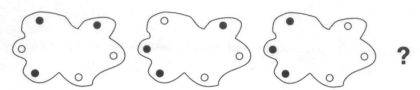

What comes next?

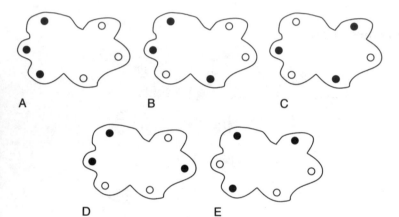

6

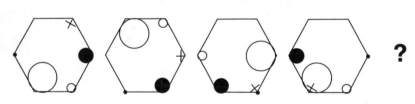

What comes next?

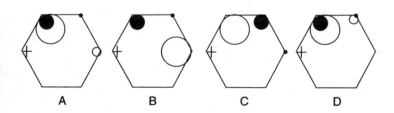

7

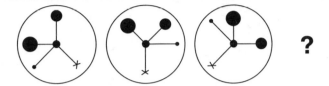

What comes next?

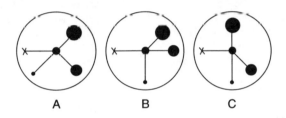

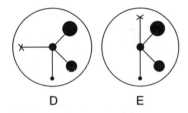

8

What comes next?

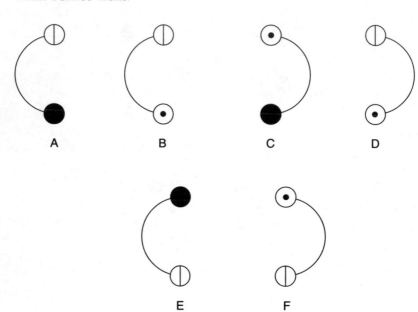

9

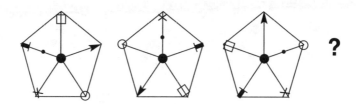

?

What comes next?

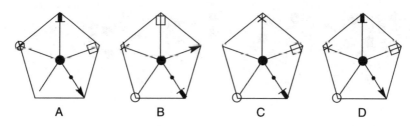

10

?

What comes next?

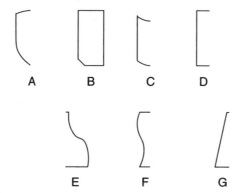

11

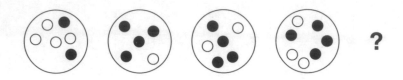

What comes next?

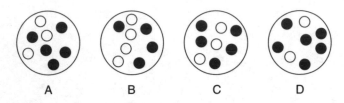

12

Complete the next square in the above sequence.

13

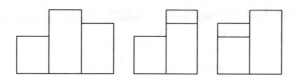

What comes next?

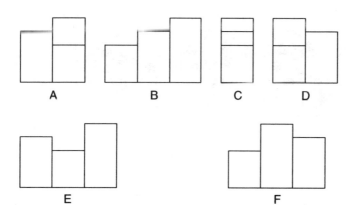

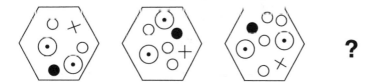

14

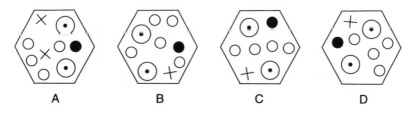

15

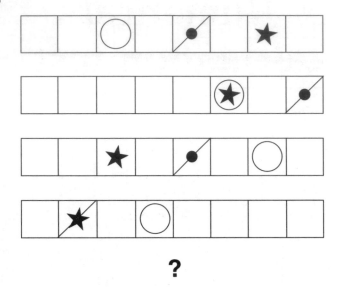

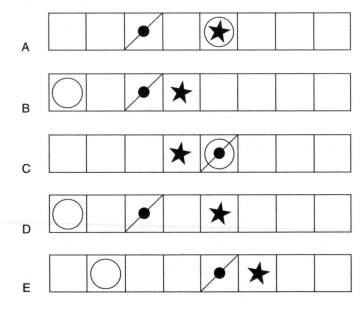

What comes next?

Numerical calculation test

1   What number should replace the question mark?

A	B	C	D
21	16	41	81
27	24	43	100
35	36	47	?
45	48	51	144
63	56	53	169

2   What weight will replace the question mark and balance the scale?

3   What number should replace the question mark?

48	6	13	21
60	10	15	21
33	11	16	19
42	14	17	20
72	12	14	?

4   Change this recurring decimal to a fraction:

.72161616 . . . (16 recurring)

5   Simplify this fraction:

$$\frac{21}{26} \quad / \quad \frac{7}{13} \quad / \quad \frac{4}{8} \quad = \quad x$$

/ indicates division

6   If
Bill's age plus Jim's age equals 121 and
Bill's age plus Arthur's age equals 112 and
Jim's age plus Arthur's age equals 57,
how old are Bill, Jim and Arthur?

7   What number continues this sequence?

59, 73, 83, 94, 107, ?

8   On a recent shopping trip the amount spent by my
     daughter was the same as the amount spent by my wife
     divided by the amount spent by myself. My wife spent
     £60 and would have spent 15 times as much as myself if
     she had spent 25% more. How much did we all spend?

9   Midway through his round a golfer hits a 203-yard drive
     which brings his average length per drive for the round
     up to now from 176 to 179 yards. How far would he
     have had to hit the drive to bring his average length of
     drive up from 176 to 181 yards?

10   Cherie has a third as many as Tony who has a third as
     many again as Gordon. Altogether they have 185. How
     many has each?

11   How many minutes is it after 12 noon if 22 minutes ago
     it was three times as many minutes after 11 a.m.?

12   A train travelling at a speed of 45 m.p.h. enters a tunnel
     that is 2.5 miles long. The length of the train is 1/8 mile.
     How long does it take for the train to pass through the
     tunnel, from the moment the front enters to the
     moment the rear emerges?

13   George and Dick share a certain sum of money in the
     ratio 4 : 5.
     If Dick has £120 how much money is shared?

14   Which number in the grid is three places away from
     itself plus 5, two places away from itself multiplied by 3,
     two places away from itself less 4, three places away
     from itself plus 2 and two places away from itself plus 7?

36	40	8	49	57	11
12	7	27	25	9	20
5	24	30	15	19	5
9	4	6	16	2	60
10	21	17	15	14	22
3	54	18	8	13	21

15   In a bag of 10 apples, three of them contain a worm.
     What are the chances of picking out just two apples and
     finding they both contain a worm?

Part two

IQ test one

1

To which shield below can a dot be added so that
both dots then meet the same conditions as in the shield
above?

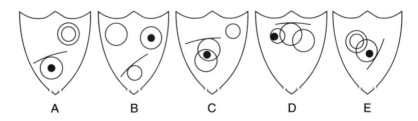

2   Which three pieces will form a perfect square when fitted together?

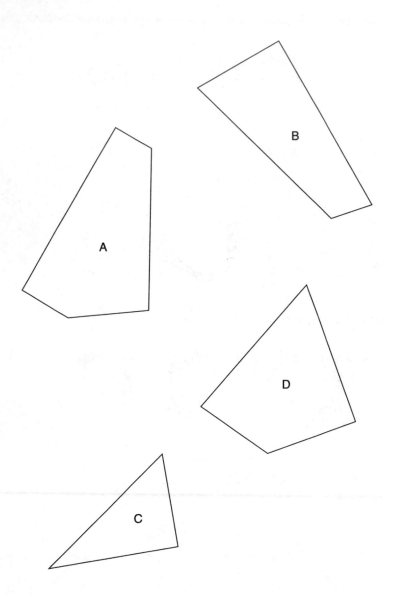

3   What number should replace the question mark?

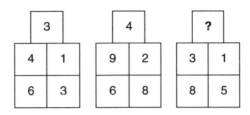

4

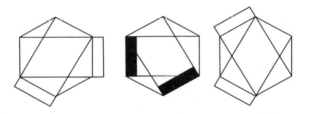

What comes next?

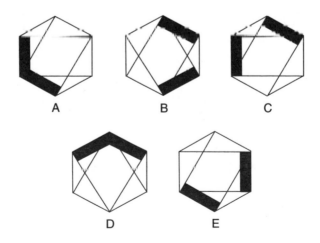

5

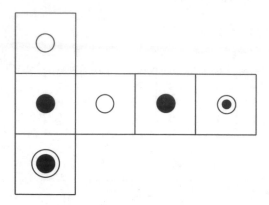

When the above is folded to form a cube, just **two** of the following can be produced. Which **two**?

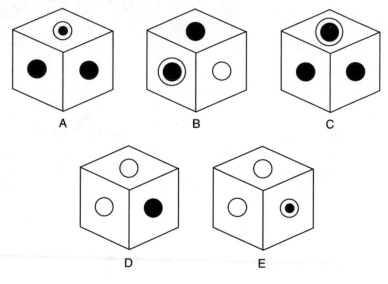

6

146, 32, 256, 31, 248, 24, ? , ?, ?

What are the next three numbers in the above sequence?

7

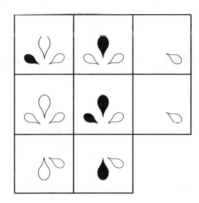

Which is the missing square?

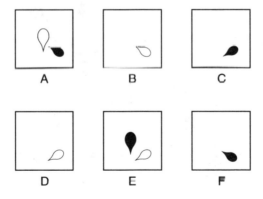

8

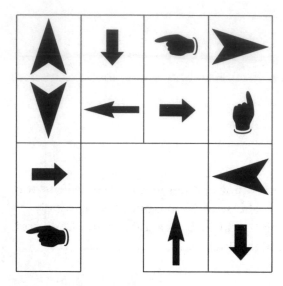

Which is the missing section?

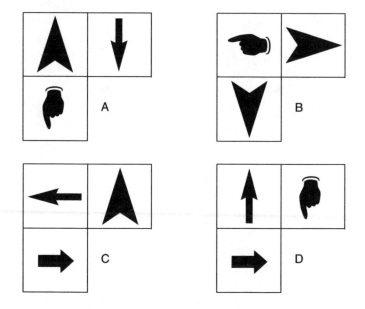

9

2	9	4	6	3
1	5	9	6	2
3	8	1	4	7
2	7	6	5	9
3	7	5	7	6

3	2	2	5	4
9	8	4	7	6
4	3	6	9	1
8	4	7	5	7
7	3	1	5	2

Find a string of four numbers that is repeated in both the left and right grids. The string may appear horizontally, vertically, diagonally, backwards or forwards in either grid, but always in a straight line.

10

Which is the missing section?

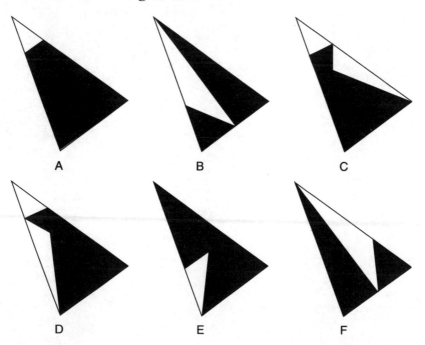

11 Which is the odd one out?

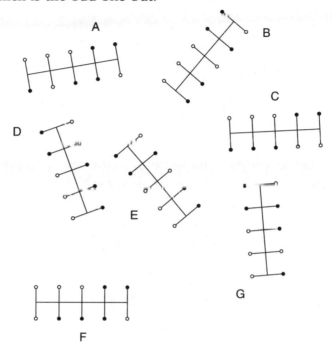

12 What number should replace the question mark?

A

25	14	11	7	61
53	9	19	12	72
17	8	23	13	49
9	21	6	?	5
31	10	15	44	1

B

75	56	55	42	427
159	36	95	72	504
51	32	115	78	343
27	84	30	60	35
93	40	75	264	7

13   What number should replace the question mark?

14   Start at a corner and spiral in to the centre to find the number to replace the question mark.

105	112	108	115	111
109	84	91	87	94
102	88	75	82	90
106	81	**?**	78	97
99	103	96	100	93

15   Multiply the smallest prime number by the largest odd number.

29	63	51	21	47	65
61	87	85	73	45	41
49	95	31	55	93	83
79	43	15	91	59	27
35	77	67	19	71	23
37	81	99	53	19	33

16

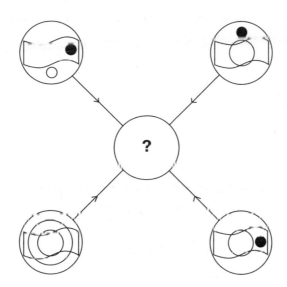

Each line and symbol that appears in the four outer circles above is to be transferred to the centre circle according to these rules. If a line or symbol occurs in the outer circles:

once	it is transferred
twice	it is possibly transferred
three times	it is transferred
four times	it is not transferred

Which of the circles A, B, C, D or E shown below should appear at the centre of the diagram above?

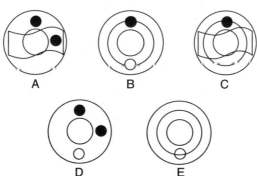

17   Which hexagon should replace the question mark?

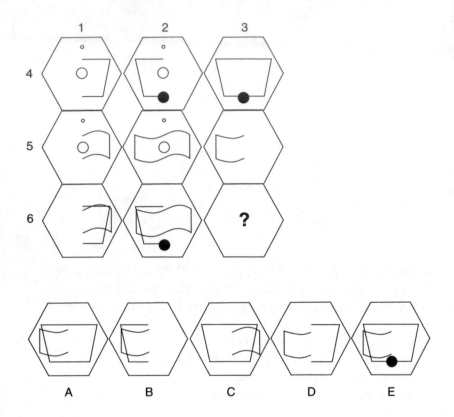

18

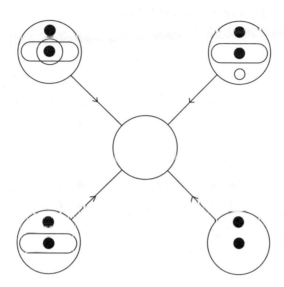

Each line and symbol that appears in the four outer circles above is to be transferred to the centre circle according to these rules. If a line or symbol occurs in the outer circles:

once	it is transferred
twice	it is possibly transferred
three times	it is transferred
four times	it is not transferred

Which of the circles A, B, C, D or E shown below should appear at the centre of the diagram above?

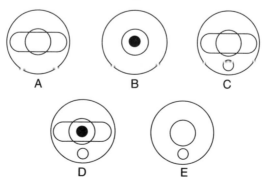

19   Which domino is the odd one out?

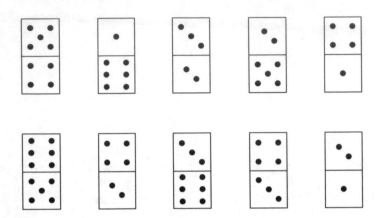

20   Which number should replace the question mark?

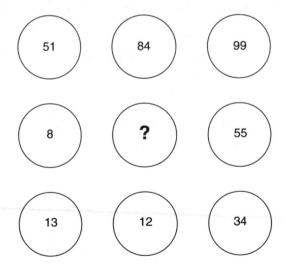

IQ test two

1

Complete the next square in the above sequence.

2

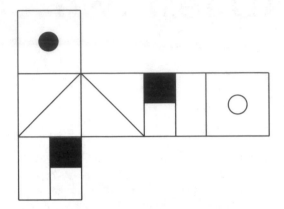

When the above is folded to form a cube, just one of the following can be produced. Which one?

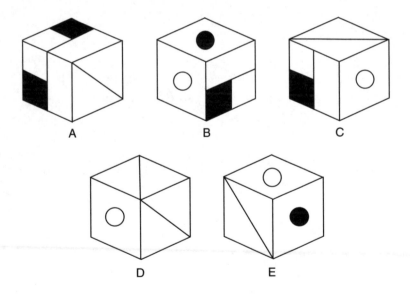

3   What number should replace the question mark?

4   Which three pieces below, when fitted together, will form a perfect square?

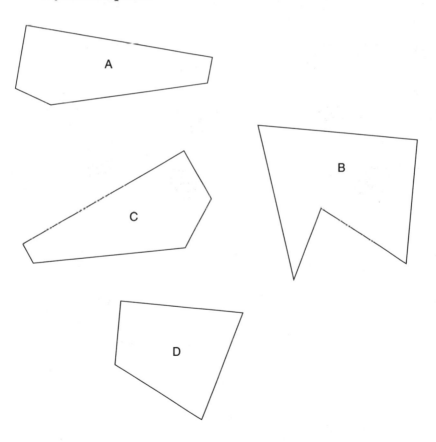

5   What number should replace the question mark?

3	6	3	9	4	?	6

7	4	2	5	4	8	1	7

6

   is to

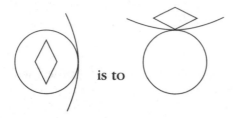

as: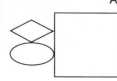

is to:

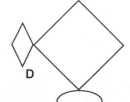   A

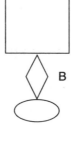   B

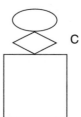   C

D   E

7 How many lines appear below?

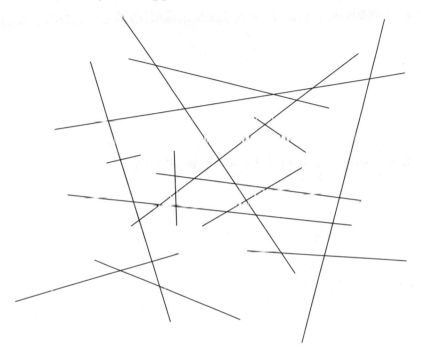

8 Which two numbers are the odd ones out?

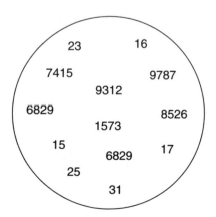

9

Which shield is most like the shield above?

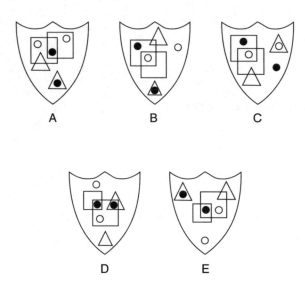

10

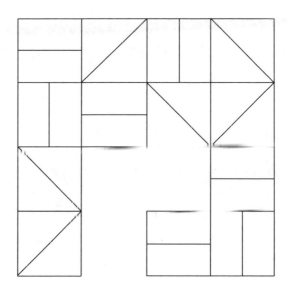

Which is the missing section?

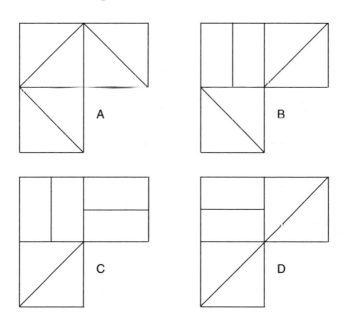

11

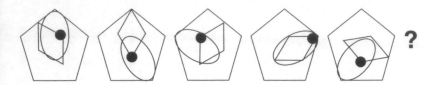

Which pentagon should come next?

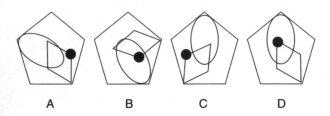

A   B   C   D

12   What is the weight of a sack of potatoes if it weighs:

A   50kg plus $\frac{1}{11}$th of its own weight?

B   55kg plus $\frac{1}{6}$th of its own weight?

C   63kg plus $\frac{1}{8}$th of its own weight?

D   88kg plus $\frac{1}{9}$th of its own weight?

There are four different answers to find.

13   What number should replace the question mark?

A

88	65	69	51	72
91	54	56	62	80
67	67	80	68	70
72	74	98	66	128
63	129	67	67	112

B

41	17	20	1	21
44	6	7	12	29
20	19	31	18	19
25	?	49	16	77
16	81	18	17	61

14   I am four times as old as my son. In 20 years' time,
     I shall be twice as old as him. How old are we today?

15   Which 5 numerals will add up to 1,000?

373	135	30	375
126	411	416	64
73	382	66	128
418	21	23	425

16 What number should replace the question mark to
    provide the missing link?

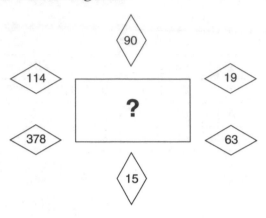

17

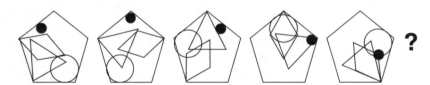

Which letter should come next?

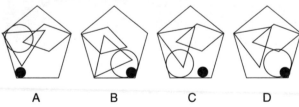

   A   B   C   D

18

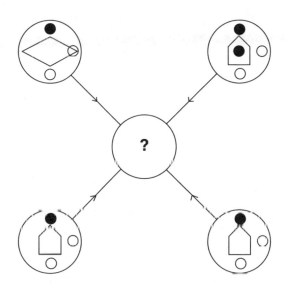

Each line and symbol that appears in the four outer circles above is to be transferred to the centre circle according to these rules. If a line or symbol occurs in the outer circles:

once   it is transferred
twice   it is possibly transferred
three times it is transferred
four times   it is not transferred

Which of the circles A, B, C, D or E shown below should appear at the centre of the diagram above?

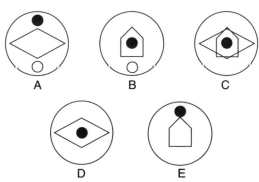

19

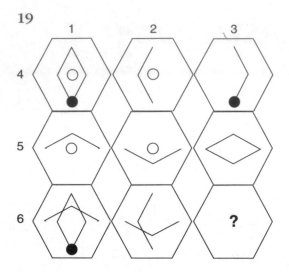

Which hexagon should replace the question mark?

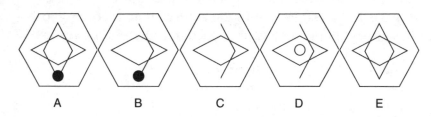

A   B   C   D   E

20   Given that each block is the total of the two blocks
      below it, fill in the boxes. There is one negative number.

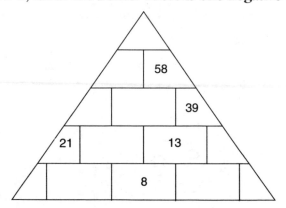

IQ test three

1

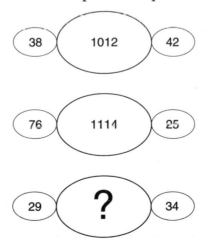

What comes next?

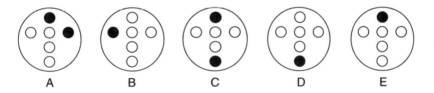

2 What number should replace the question mark?

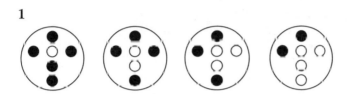

3

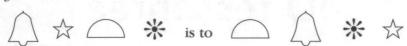 is to

as

is to

A

B

C

D

E

4

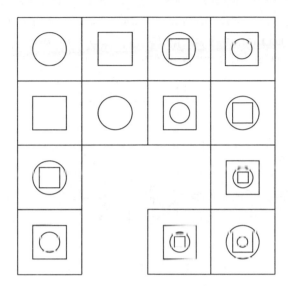

Which is the missing section?

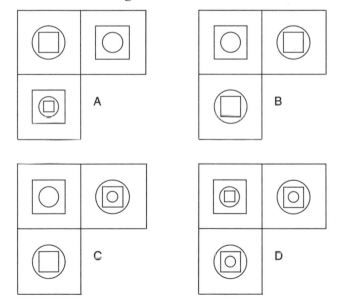

5 472, 314, 723, ?

What number continues the sequence?

6 Divide the square into four pieces of equal size and shape so that each of the four pieces contains one each of the four different symbols.

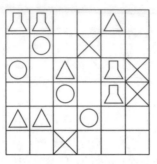

7

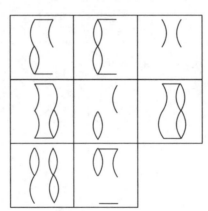

Which is the missing square?

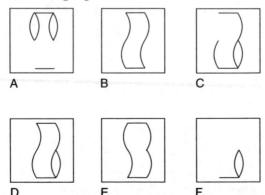

A   B   C

D   E   F

8

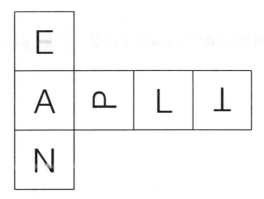

When the above is folded to form a cube, just one of the
following can be produced. Which one?

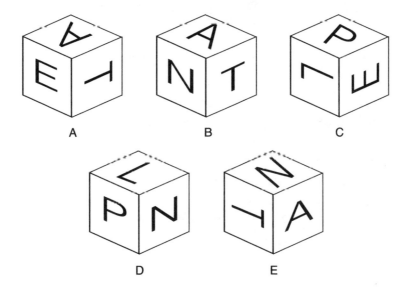

9   What number should replace the question mark?

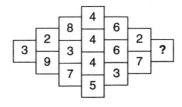

10

Which two figures come next?

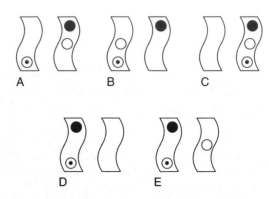

11   Which of these calculations does not equal 100?

    A $47^9/_{16} + 52^7/_{16}$

    B $12^2 - 70 + (2 \times 13)$

    C $3^2 + 4^2 + 5^2 + 6^2 + 64 - 56$

    D $100 \times {}^{13}/_{17} \div {}^{26}/_{34}$

12   Six pineapples and eight Ugli fruit costs 200p.
    Five pineapples and 10 Ugli fruit costs 190p.
    How much does one pineapple cost, and one Ugli fruit?

13

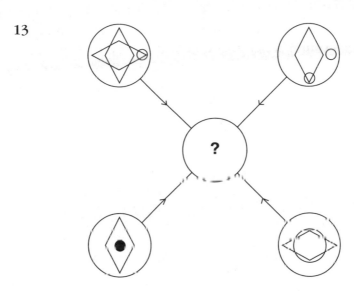

Each line and symbol that appears in the four outer circles above is to be transferred to the centre circle according to these rules. If a line or symbol occurs in the outer circles:

once: it is transferred
twice: it is possibly transferred
three times: it is transferred
four times: It is not transferred.

Which of the circles A, B, C, D or E shown below should appear at the centre of the diagram above?

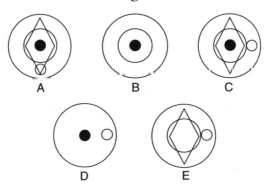

14   In how many ways can you take one number from each of the 3 columns that together will add up to 20?

10	8	1
7	17	9
5	6	7
6	9	4
2	11	8

15   What number should replace the question mark?

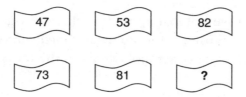

16   The letters A to H equal the numbers 1 to 8 but not in that order. Find the values of each letter if:

$$B + D = 3$$

$$A + F = 8$$

$$C + G = 15$$

$$D + H = 7$$

$$B + E = 6$$

$$C + F = 10$$

$$B + E + G = 14$$

Hint: A = 5

17 Simplify $^{17}/_{23} \div {}^{8}/_{46} \div {}^{34}/_{16}$

18 What number should replace the question mark?

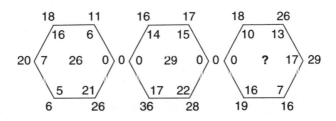

19 What number comes next?

20 What number should replace the question mark?

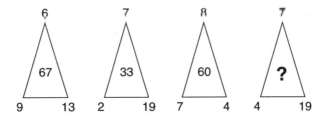

IQ test four

1

A B C D E F G H

What letter is three to the right of the letter that is immediately to the left of the letter that comes midway between the letter immediately to the left of the letter H and the letter two places to the left of the letter C?

2

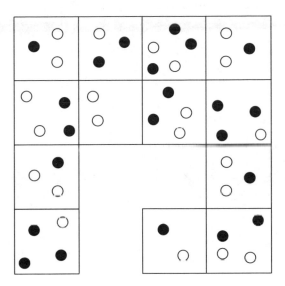

Which is the missing section?

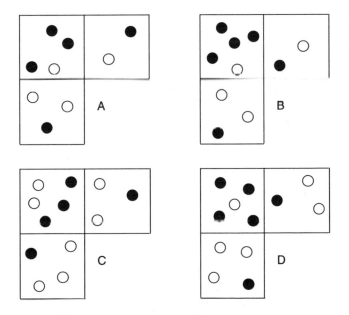

3

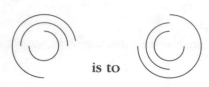

is to

as

is to

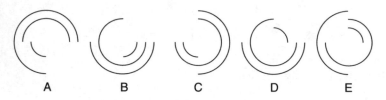

| A | B | C | D | E |

4   Complete the four missing numbers:

3	8	4	9	6	3
6	4	8	6	9	8
9	9	?	?	4	4
4	6	?	?	8	9
8	3	9	4	3	6
3	8	4	9	6	3

5   Which is the odd one out?

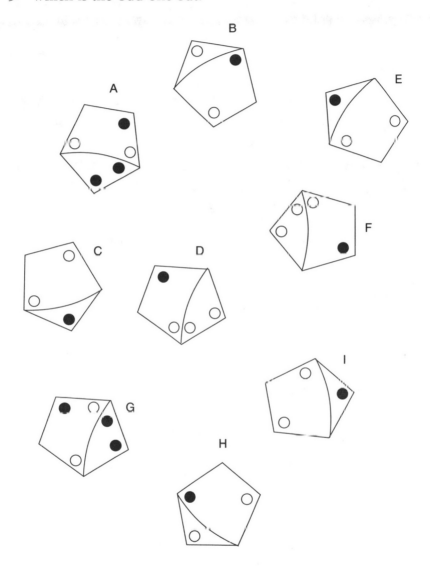

6

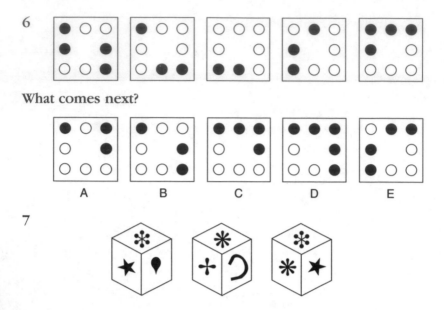

What comes next?

A   B   C   D   E

7

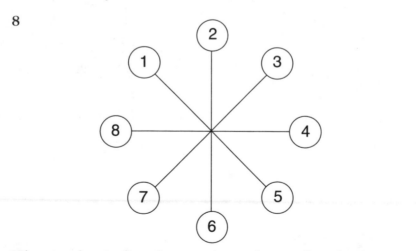

Three views of the same cube are shown. What symbol is opposite the ✳

8

What number is directly opposite to the number that is two places clockwise from the number that is directly opposite the number that is three places anti-clockwise from the number four?

9

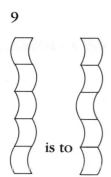

is to

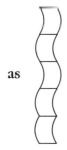

as

is to

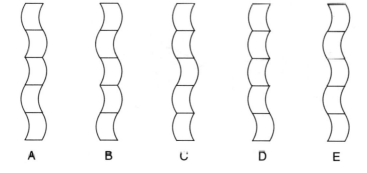

A   B   C   D   E

10

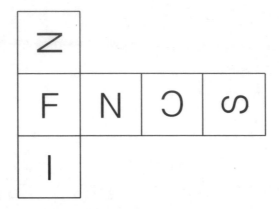

When the above is folded to form a cube, just one of the following can be produced. Which one?

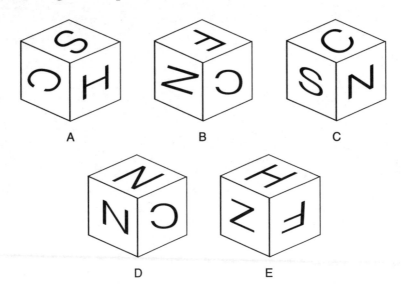

11   Which hexagon replaces the question mark?

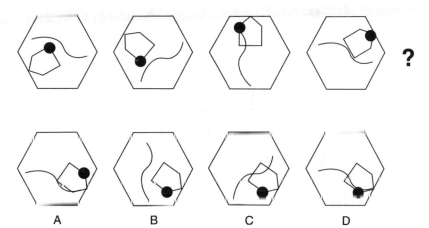

?

A   B   C   D

12

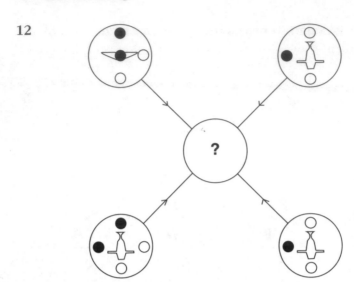

Each line and symbol that appears in the four outer circles above is to be transferred to the centre circle according to these rules. If a line or symbol occurs in the outer circles:

once   it is transferred
twice   it is possibly transferred
three times it is transferred
four times   it is not transferred.

Which of the circles A, B, C, D or E shown below should appear at the centre of the diagram above?

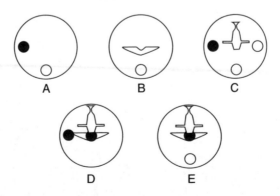

13 Each block in this pyramid is the total of the two blocks below it. Can you find all of the missing numbers?

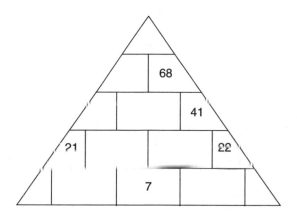

14 Which pair of balls is the odd one out?

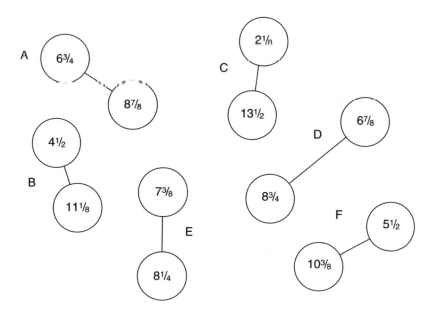

15   How many triangles are in this diagram?

16   What number should replace the question mark?

11		9
	76	
17		7

13		11
	44	
17		11

27		31
	?	
14		8

17   Five murder suspects are being questioned. In their five statements, only three of them tell the truth. Who is the murderer?

Arthur says: 'Derek is the murderer.'

Bill says: 'I am innocent.'

Charlie says: 'It wasn't Edward.'

Derek says: 'Arthur is lying.'

Edward says, 'Bill is telling the truth.'

18   Which is the odd one out?

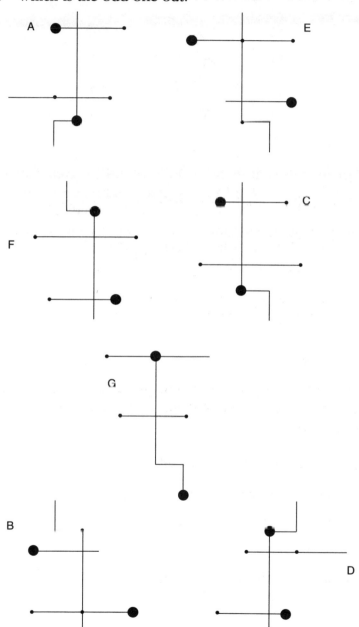

19   Which four of these numbers will add up to 500?

34	225	46	97
119	26	21	2
71	88	16	76
112	179	80	80

20   The first five batsmen – A, B, C, D and E – averaged 40
runs each. D scored 12. A was the highest scorer. B and
D scored 28 between them. C and E scored 72 between
them. C scored ten more than E. D scored four fewer
than B. B, C and D scored 69 between them. How many
did each batsman score?

IQ test five

1

To which square below can a dot be added so that it then meets the same conditions as in the box above?

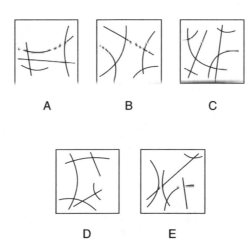

A   B   C

D   E

2   Which circle should replace the question mark?

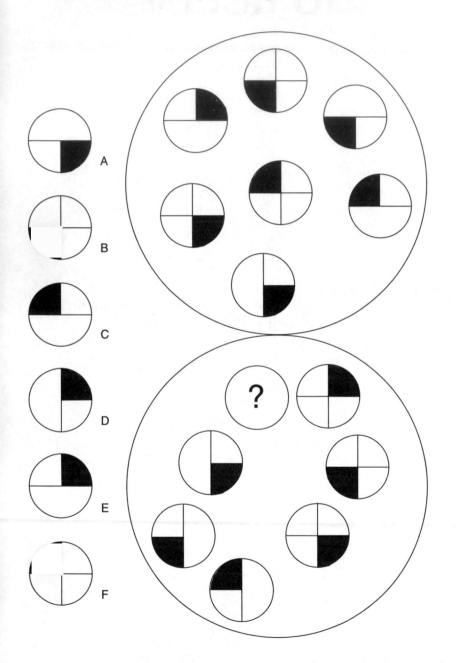

3 If a man and a half build a wall and a half in a day and a half, how many walls will six men build in six days?

4

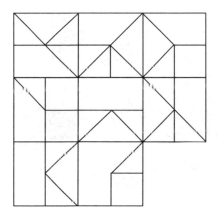

Which is the missing square?

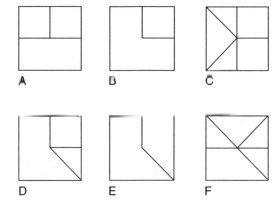

5   How many circles contain a black dot?

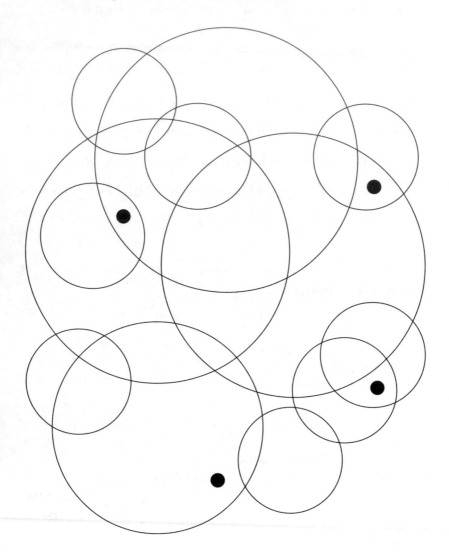

6

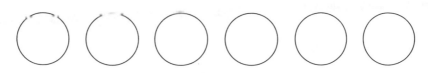

Arrange the numbers 1 to 6 in the circles in such a way that:

Numbers 1 and 2 and all the digits between them add up to 8

Numbers 2 and 3 and all the digits between them add up to 11

Numbers 3 and 4 and all the digits between them add up to 21

Numbers 4 and 5 and all the digits between them add up to 17

7

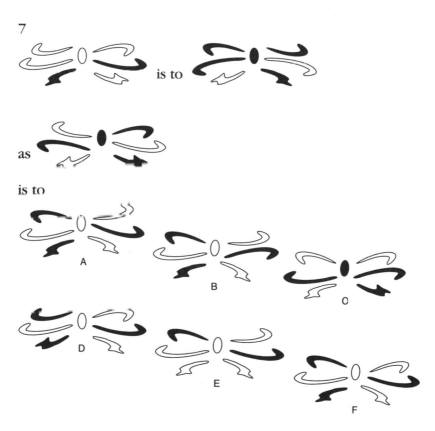

8

What comes next?

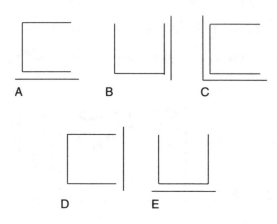

9   A man has 53 socks in his drawer; 29 identical blue, 17 identical red and seven identical black. The lights have fused and he is completely in the dark. How many socks must he take out to make 100 per cent certain that he has one pair of each colour?

10

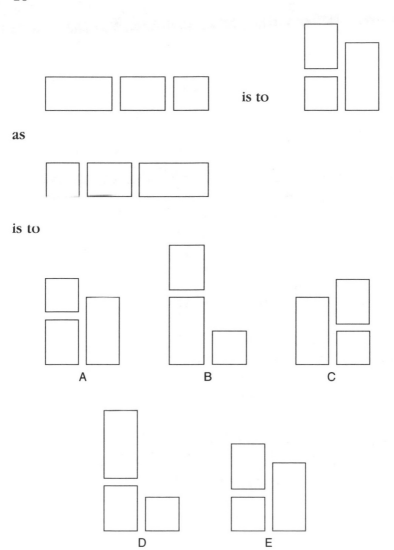

11

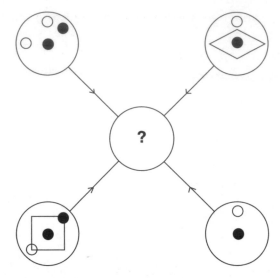

Each line and symbol that appears in the four outer circles above is to be transferred to the centre circle according to these rules. If a line or symbol occurs in the outer circles:

once   it is transferred
twice   it is possibly transferred
three times   it is transferred
four times   it is not transferred.

Which of the circles A, B, C, D or E shown below should appear at the centre of the diagram above?

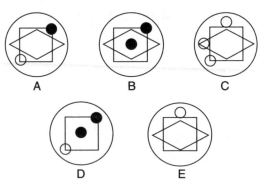

12   What number should replace the question mark?

16   39   85   177   361   ?

13

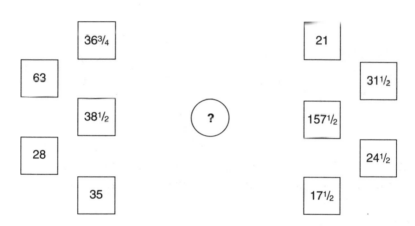

Place the smallest number in the centre by which all of the outside numbers can be divided exactly. The correct answer is greater than one, and is not a whole number.

14   Which of these calculations does not total 85?

A $18/9 \div 8/330$

B $6^2 + 7^2$

C   1010101 (binary)

D   LXXXV (Roman)

E $2295/27$

15   Which of these calculations does not equal 512?

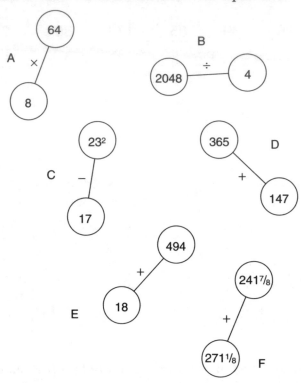

16   What number should replace the question mark?

56   67   80   88   104   ?

17   Start at a corner and spiral in to the centre to find the
number to replace the question mark.

40	45	35	40	30
50	75	80	70	75
45	85	90	95	65
55	80	90	?	70
50	60	55	65	60

18 Can you work out the value of the four symbols?

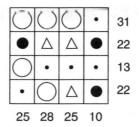

◡	◡	◯	•	31
●	△	△	●	22
◯	•	•	•	13
•	◯	△	●	22

25 28 25 10

19 Which hexagon should replace the question mark?

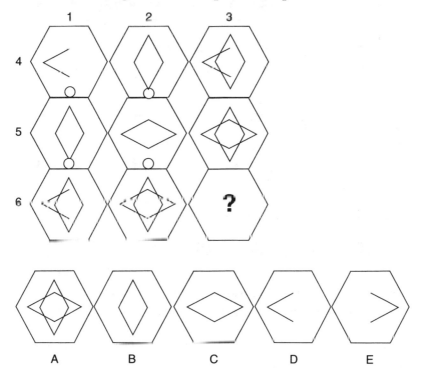

20

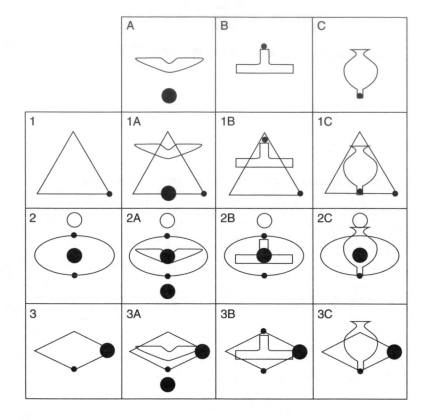

Each of the nine squares in the grid marked 1A to 3C should incorporate all the lines and symbols that are shown in the squares of the same letter and number at the top of the column and at the end of the row to the extreme left of them. For example, 2B should incorporate all the lines and symbols that are in 2 and B. One of the squares is incorrect. Which one is it?

IQ test six

1

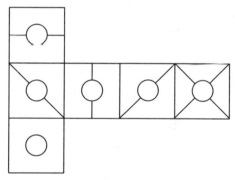

When the above is folded to form a cube, just one of the
following can be produced. Which one?

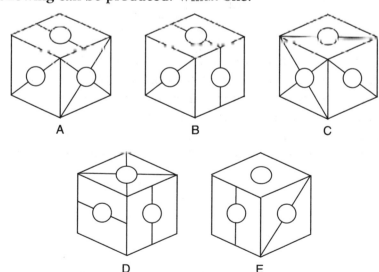

2

— — — — — —

— | — — — —

— — | — — —

— | — | — —

— — | — | —

What comes next?

A　— | — | — —

B　— — | — | —

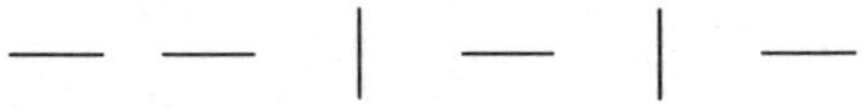

C　— | — | — |

D　| — | — | —

E　— — — | — |

F　— — | — — |

3

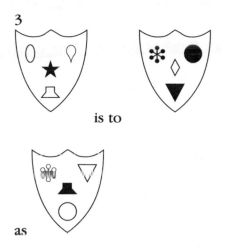

is to

as

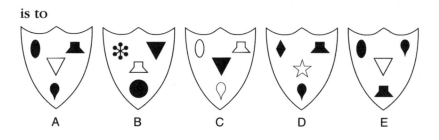

is to

4

SUNDAY
MONDAY
TUESDAY
WEDNESDAY
THURSDAY
FRIDAY
SATURDAY

What day comes immediately before the day that comes two days after the day that comes four days before the day that comes immediately after Thursday?

5

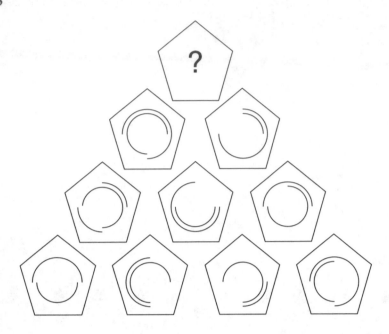

Which pentagon should replace the question mark?

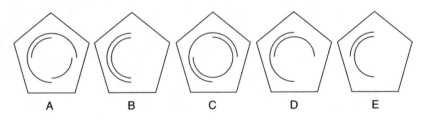

A   B   C   D   E

6 Which three pieces below will form a perfect circle when fitted together?

7   What number should replace the question mark?

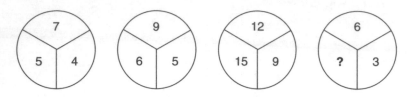

8

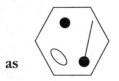   is to

as

is to

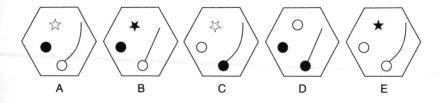

9   What number should replace the question mark?

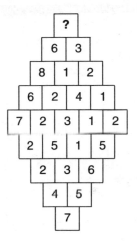

10

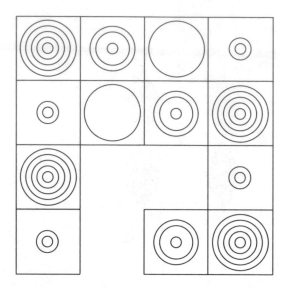

Which is the missing section?

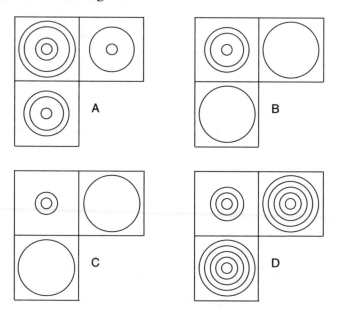

11

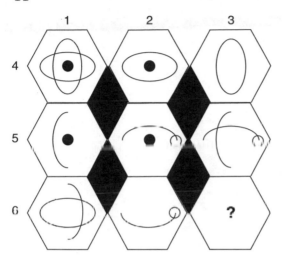

Which hexagon should replace the question mark?

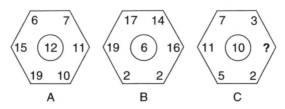

12   The ages of two friends, when added together, make 63.
     One said, 'I am twice as old as you were when I was as
     old as you are now.' Find their ages.

13   What number should replace the question mark?

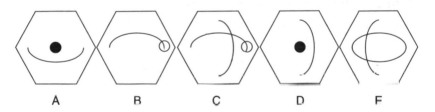

14 What number should replace the question mark?

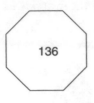

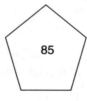

15 How many revolutions must the large cog make to return all the cogs to their starting position?

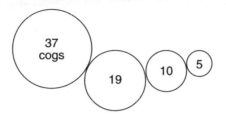

16 In how many ways can these three digits be arranged to produce a three-digit number?

762

17

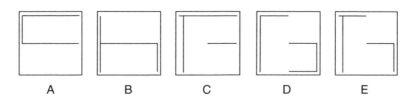

Which square should replace the question mark?

18 What number should replace the question mark?

13 – 73 – 14 – 34 – 74 – 35 – 95 – **?**

19

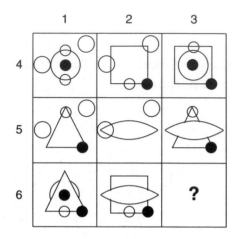

Which of these tiles will fit logically into the empty space?

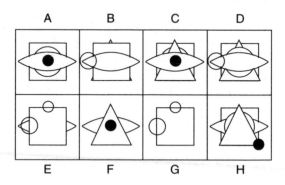

20

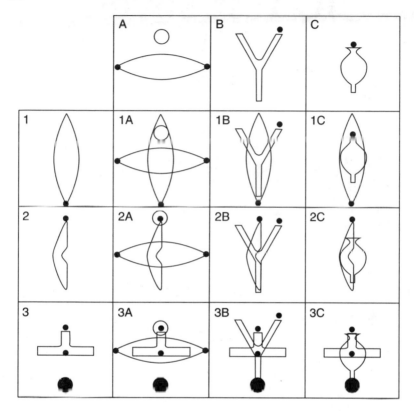

Each of the nine squares in the grid marked 1A to 3C should incorporate all the lines and symbols that are shown in the squares of the same letter and number at the top of the column and at the end of the row to the extreme left of them. For example, 2B should incorporate all the lines and symbols that are in 2 and B. One of the squares is incorrect. Which one is it?

IQ test seven

1

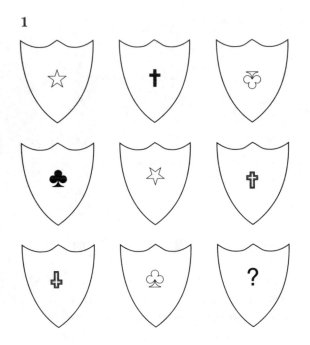

Which shield should replace the question mark?

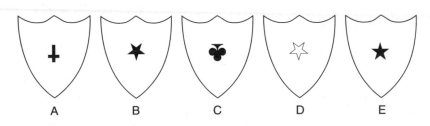

2   How many lines appear below?

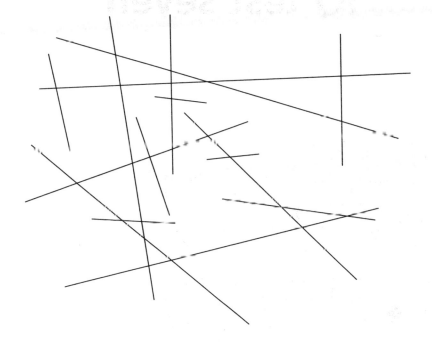

3

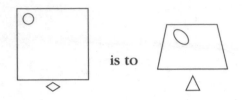

is to

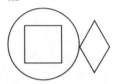

as

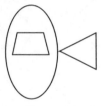

is to

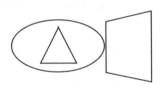

A   B   C

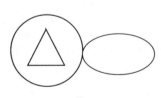      

D   E

4   What number should replace the question mark?

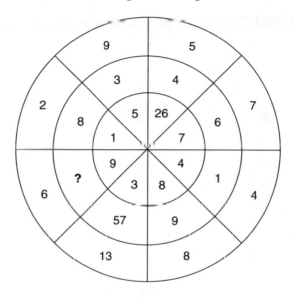

5

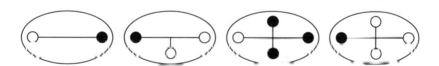

Draw the next ellipse in the above sequence.

6

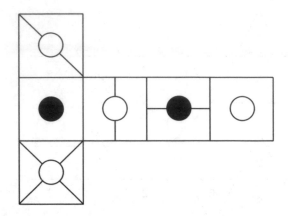

When the above is folded to form a cube, just one of the following can be produced. Which one?

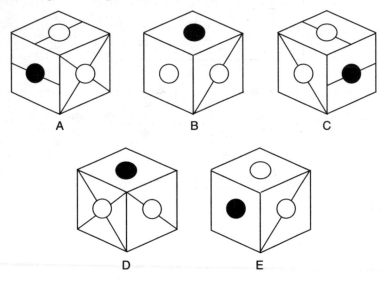

7 What number should replace the question mark?

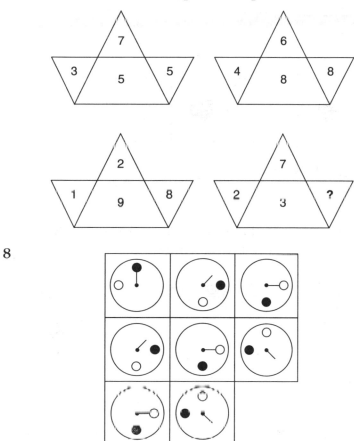

8

Which is the missing square?

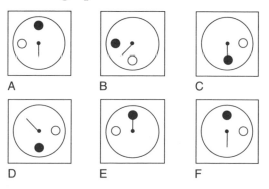

A   B   C

D   E   F

9

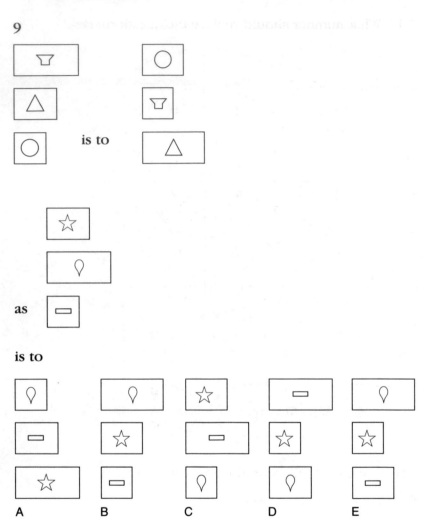

as

is to

A   B   C   D   E

10

12	21	49	38
46	20	14	27
28	53	30	15
65	32	8	18

13	23	3	2
19	6	17	16
1	17	24	11
21	4	8	15

Multiply the third highest even number in the left-hand grid by the third lowest odd number in the right-hand grid.

11

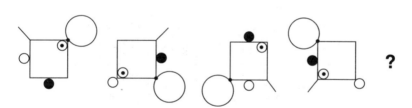

Which diagram should replace the question mark?

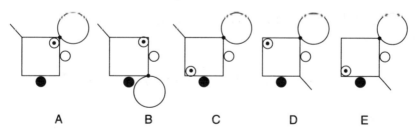

| A | B | C | D | E |

12

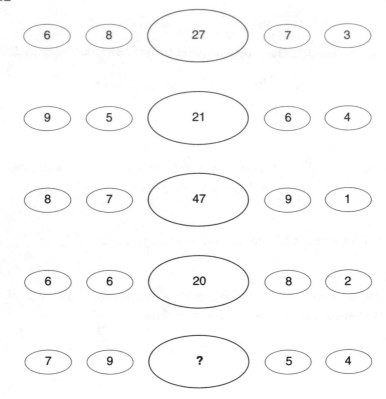

What number should replace the question mark?

13

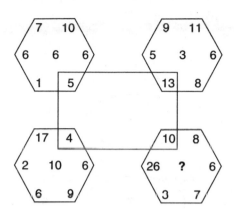

What number should replace the question mark?

14 All the mathematical symbols have been omitted from
    this sum. See if you can replace them.

81   9   17   6   59   =   100

15

What number should replace the question mark?

16 What is the sum of the numbers that are consecutive among the following?

27	35	6	41
19	55	47	20
38	12	90	28
49	31	53	86
7	30	13	39
89	42	21	36

17

A

9	26	10	4	15
12	2	16	14	7
1	22	6	21	23
13	19	3	18	20
8	17	24	9	11

B

26	10	27	34	24
23	34	21	24	32
34	14	31	17	16
22	17	34	?	19
27	19	13	29	28

What number should replace the question mark?

18 What number should replace the question mark?

17   23³/₄   **?**   37¹/₄   44

19

If

then

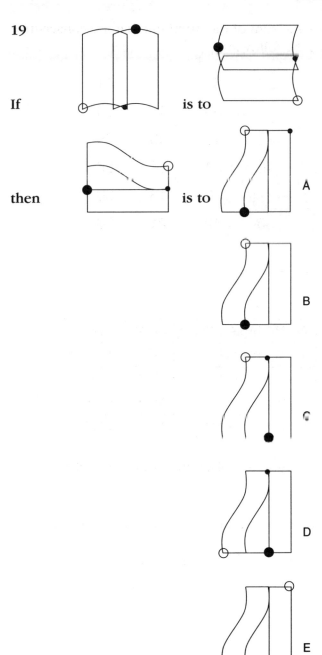

20

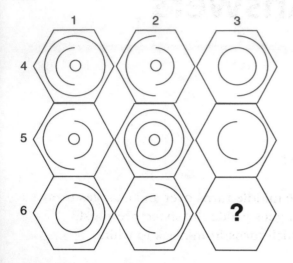

Which hexagon should replace the question mark?

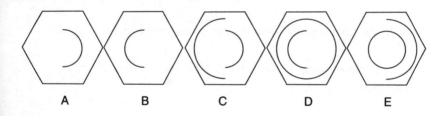

Answers

Visual analogy test

1 B; the shape in the middle turns over and changes from white to black and goes inside the shape previously surrounding it, which turns from black to white.

2 F; the number of sides in the original figure reduces by one from seven to six. The number of dots increases from three to four and they change from white to black.

3 C; lines turn upside down and circles turn upside down.

4 C; the large circle moves 180°. The two centre circles lose dots and move 180°.

5 D; the diamond moves 90° and increases in size. The triangle increases in size and goes inside the diamond. The rectangle decreases in size, rotates 90° and goes on top of the diamond.

6 B; the figure flips over and individual components in the same position as in the original analogy change places and reverse black and white as in the original analogy.

7 B; four black dots change to three black dots. Three white dots change to four white dots.

8   B; add the number of black dots and take the difference in the number of white dots in the first two figures to arrive at the number of dots in the final figure.

9   C; two white dots change to three white dots.

10   C; the figure flips over from top to bottom and only the inner lines disappear.

11   A; figures originally inside the figure change to outside the figure and from black to white; and vice versa.

12   A; the large square changes to a large circle. The small square changes to a small circle. The small triangle changes to a large triangle. The oval moves 45° or 315°.

13   C; the top white circle changes to black. The middle circle changes to white. The bottom circle changes to black.

14   B; the figure moves 90° clockwise with black/white reversal of the spikes.

15   A; the semicircle moves 180°. The centre circle changes to white.

Assessment

14 – 15 Exceptional
11 – 12 Excellent
 9 – 10 Very good
 7 – 8 Good
 5 – 6 Average

Visual odd one out test

1   C; A is similar to E and B is similar to D with black/white reversal.

2   C; the rest only form two triangles. Four triangles in total are formed by the arrangement of lines in C.

3   G; A and C are the same, as are B and F, and D and E.

4   B; D and E are the same, as are A and C, and G and F.

5   D; the only one where two black dots are directly connected.

6   G; B and F are the same, as are D and E, and A and C.

7   D; in all the others a figure with an odd number of sides is black and a figure with an even number of sides is white.

8   E; in all the others an arrow points left to a black figure and an arrow points right to a white figure.

9   F; A and G are the same, as are C and E, and B and D.

10 B; A is the same as E, and C is the same as D.

11 F; in all the others a mark at the bottom, i.e. below the straight line, points to a gap at the top.

12 A; C and G are the same, as are B and D, and F and E.

13 D; the only straight-sided figure to have an arrow pointing at it.

14   A; it is made up of six lines whereas the remainder are made up of seven lines.

15   A; it is the only diagram to produce an odd number of triangles, i.e. five. B produces 10 triangles, C produces eight, D produces six and E produces four.

Assessment

14 – 15 Exceptional
11 – 12 Excellent
 9 – 10 Very Good
 7 – 8   Good
 5 – 6   Average

Lateral thinking test

1   7; numbers in the middle square are the sum of numbers in the same positions in the other two squares. So, 5 + 2 = 7.

2   D; each circle is obtained by joining together the two circles below, however, similar symbols disappear.

3   8; each pyramidal group of three numbers totals 17.

4   K; the termination of letters is 3, 4, 3, 4, 3, 4 i.e. F = 3 terminations as illustrated below:

5   He knew door number 7 was faulty, otherwise the supervisor would have said, 'Three doors out of the first six are faulty.'

6   Z; all contain 3 lines, i.e. H N Y F K (Z).

7   D; looking across and down the contents of the third circle are determined by the contents of the first two circles. Looking at sections in the same position, two whites = black, two blacks = white, and black + white = white.

8   D; there is one each of the four different symbols in each horizontal and vertical line i.e. one large white circle, two medium size white circles (one with a small white circle above it) and one black circle.

9   B; each line of squares contains ten white and seven black circles.

10   E; looking across and down, two white circles in the same position in the first two squares equals a black circle in the same position in the third square, and vice versa; but black and white in the same position equals a blank in the third square.

11   R; all the letters listed have enclosed areas.

12   D; only when a black or white circle appears in the same position three times in the surrounding circles is it transferred to the circle in the middle.

13   375 stripes. As 15 is one-third of 45, by taking out two-thirds of the female fish you are effectively leaving all the original fish with 15 stripes, so $25 \times 15 = 375$ stripes.

For example say 15 female + 10 male. Then this leaves

$$5 \text{ female} \times 45 = 225$$
$$10 \text{ male} \times 15 = \underline{150} \quad +$$
$$= 375$$

14   1; each number represents the number of other numbers adjacent either vertically, horizontally or diagonally.

15   It is impossible. In the first half of the journey I have used up all the time required to achieve 20 m.p.h. average speed.

Assessment

19 – 20 Exceptional
16 – 18 Excellent
13 – 15 Very good
10 – 12 Good
 6 – 9   Average

Which letter comes next test

1 S   2 Q   3 F   4 Z   5 N   6 E   7 R

8 U   9 L   10 Y   11 I   12 H   13 A   14 N

15 M

Assessment

14 – 15 Exceptional
11 – 12 Excellent
 9 – 10 Very Good
 7 – 8   Good
 5 – 6   Average

Visual sequence test

1

Looking across, the eyes alternate squint/forward/left; the
nose alternates black/white and the mouth alternates
happy/sad/straight.

2 D; the large circle moves 90° clockwise, the small circle
   180°, the black dot 90° clockwise and the line 90°
   clockwise.

3 D; the diamond next to the end always moves to the
   front and the diamond third from the front always moves
   to the end.

4   C; the arrow moves two corners clockwise, the large circle three corners clockwise, the black dot three corners anti-clockwise, the longer line one corner clockwise and the shorter line one corner clockwise.

5   A; the dots are changing places two at a time working clockwise, starting with the white dot on the extreme left, which changes places with the black dot immediately above it.

6   D; the large white circle moves two corners clockwise, the black circle moves one corner clockwise, the small white circle moves two corners anti-clockwise, the black dot moves one corner anti-clockwise and the cross moves one corner clockwise.

7   D; the large black circle moves 45° clockwise, the small black circle moves 45° clockwise, the black dot moves 135° anti-clockwise and the cross moves 45° clockwise.

8   D; at each stage the main figure rotates through 180° and the circle orginally at the bottom at stage 1 alternates white/dot in middle/black.

9   D; the square moves two corners clockwise, the arrow moves two corners clockwise, the circle moves two corners clockwise, the rectangle moves two corners clockwise, the black dot moves one line clockwise and the cross moves two corners clockwise.

10 D; the first four figures are being repeated, but only the left-hand half.

11 B; black dots are worth two points and white dots one point. The score progresses 8 – 9 – 10 – 11. B is thus valued at 12. A and C are 13 and D is 14.

12

The shaded portion moves in the sequence 1, 2, 3, 2, 1 as shown below.

13   E; the segment originally at the extreme right is moving right to left at each stage.

14   B; at each stage the number of small white circles increases by 1.

15   D; at each stage each of the three individual symbols is moving left to right then right to left i.e. count three spaces forward then three back including turns on reaching the end of a line.

Assessment

14 – 15   Exceptional
11 – 12   Excellent
 9 – 10   Very Good
 7 – 8   Good
 5 – 6   Average

Numerical calculation test

1 121
 Column A = odd numbers
 Column B = even numbers
 Column C = prime numbers
 Column D = square numbers ($11^2 = 121$)

2 7 Kg

Left Hand		Right Hand	
8 Kg × 4 = 32		7 Kg × 3 = 21	
7 Kg × 7 = $\underline{49}$	+	10 Kg × 6 = $\underline{60}$	+
81		81	

3 20
 48/6 + 13 = 21
 60/10 + 15 = 21
 33/11 + 16 = 19
 42/14 + 17 = 20
 72/12 + 14 = 20

4 $\dfrac{71.44}{99}$

 1 = .72161616 . . .
 $\dfrac{100}{99} = \dfrac{72.16161616 \ldots}{71.44}$

5 3

 $\dfrac{21}{26} \times \dfrac{13}{7} \times \dfrac{8}{4}$

6 Bill = 88, Jim = 33, Arthur = 24

7   115
$$59 + 5 + 9 = 73$$
$$73 + 7 + 3 = 83$$
$$83 + 8 + 3 = 94$$
$$94 + 9 + 4 = 107$$
$$107 + 1 + 7 = 115$$

8   My wife £60, daughter £12, myself £5.
$$60 + (25\% \text{ of } 60) = 75$$
$$5 \times 15 = 75$$

9   221 yards
8 holes average 176 = 1,408 yards
9 holes average 179 = 1,611 yards
9 holes average 181 = 1,629 yards

$$1,408 - 1,629 = 221 \text{ yards}$$

10   Gordon 45, Tony 60, Cherie 80

11   19 minutes
$$19 \times 3 = 57$$
57 minutes after 11 a.m. = 11.57
11.57 + 22 minutes = 12.19

12   3.5 minutes
2.5 tunnel + 0.125 train = 2.625 miles
At a speed of 45 m.p.h. the train takes $2.625 \times \dfrac{60}{45}$

to pass through the tunnel

i.e. 3.5 minutes

13   £216

Dick's share is £120 = 5 parts i.e. each part is £24
(120/5)

Therefore, the original amount was £24 × 9 parts
(4 + 5) = £216

14   6

15   17 to 1

$$\frac{3}{10} \times \frac{2}{9} = \frac{5}{90} = \frac{1}{18} \text{ or 17 to 1}$$

Assessment

14 – 15   Exceptional
11 – 12   Excellent
 9 – 10   Very Good
 7 – 8   Good
 5 – 6   Average

IQ test one

1   D; so that one dot is in the small circle only and the
    other dot is in the circle with the line above it.

2   ACD

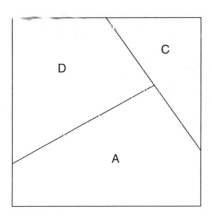

3   6
    3 + 8 + 5 = 16; similarly 4 + 6 + 3 = 13
    and 9 ׀ 7 + 8 = 24

4   C; the whole figure is rotating one side clockwise at each
    stage. The flaps alternate outside then inside the figure.
    When inside they are black.

5   B and D

6   192, 87, 696
    Take difference of alternate digits, then multiply by 8.
    So, 24 × 8 = 192, 192 produces 87 (9 – 1 = 8
    and 9 – 2 = 7), 87 × 8 = 696.

7   D; looking across the line, the contents of the third
    square are determined by the contents of the first two.
    Only when a symbol appears the same colour in the
    first two squares is it carried forward to the third
    square; however, it then appears upside down.

8   D; each line across and down contains an arrow
    pointing north, south, east and west.

9   7642 (or 2467)

10   D; starting at the bottom segment and working
     clockwise, pairs of segments have black/white reversal.

11   F
     A and G are the same, as are B and E, and C and D.

12   10
     First column in A × 3 = first column in B
     Second column in A × 4 = second column in B
     Third column in A × 5 = third column in B
     Fourth column in A × 6 = fourth column in B
     Fifth column in A × 7 = fifth column in B

13   $16\frac{3}{8}$
     $$\begin{array}{r} 5 \times 1\frac{7}{8} = \quad 9\frac{3}{8} \\ 4 \times 1\frac{3}{4} = \quad 7 \\ \hline 16\frac{3}{8} \end{array} \;+$$

14   85
     + 4 − 7 repeat; start at 111

15   1881
     19 × 99

16   B

17   E
1 is added to 2 to make 3
4 is added to 5 to make 6
but similar symbols disappear

18   C

19   4:2
Total of spots is even; but remainder are odd.

20   74
51 + 48 (84 reversed) = 99
8 + 47 (74 reversed) = 55
13 + 21 (12 reversed) = 34

Assessment

19 – 20   Exceptional
16 – 18   Excellent
13 – 15   Very good
10 – 12   Good
6 – 9   Average

IQ test two

1

Working clockwise a line appears in each segment in turn, then when two lines form a cross in each segment these lines disappear one at a time, the whole process being repeated over and over.

2   E

3   1
Take the difference in the pairs of numbers right and left to obtain the numbers top and bottom. So, difference between 8 and 5 is 3 and difference between 7 and 1 is 6.

4   ABD

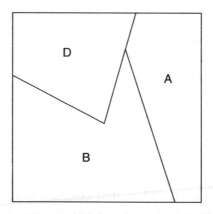

5   9

Add and subtract alternately from left to right. So,
$7 - 4 = 3, 4 + 2 = 6, 5 - 2 = 3, 5 + 4 = 9, 8 - 4 = 4,$
$8 + 1 = 9, 7 - 1 = 6$

6   C; the figures are rearranged vertically with the figure originally on the right, the diamond, now in the middle.

7   15

8   23 and 8526
The remaining numbers are in pairs where the sum of
the digits of each four figure number equals one of the
two figure numbers, e.g. 9312 (9 + 3 + 1 + 2 = 15).
The other pairs are 6829/25, 1573/16, 7415/17 and
9787/31.

9   E; it contains two triangles, two squares, two black dots
and two white dots, with one black dot in a triangle, one
black dot in both squares and one white dot in one square.

10   B; so that each horizontal and vertical line contains one
of the four different lines.

11   D
Oval moves two corners clockwise.
Diamond moves from a line to the next corner
clockwise.
Black dot moves one corner clockwise on the diamond.

12   A   55 Kg
B   66 Kg
C   72 Kg
D   99 Kg

13   26
First column in A – 47 = first column in B
Second column in A – 48 = second column in B
Third column in A – 49 = third column in B
Fourth column in A – 50 = fourth column in B
Fifth column in A – 51 = fifth column in B

14   I am 40; my son is 10. In 20 years' time, I shall be 60,
and he will be 30.

15    $416 + 373 + 126 + 64 + 21 = 1,000$

16   6

$$\frac{90}{15} \times \frac{114}{19} \times \frac{378}{63} = 6$$

17   B
Diamond moves two corners clockwise.
Triangle moves one corner clockwise.
Circle moves one corner clockwise.
Black dot moves from a line to the next corner clockwise.

18   C

19   B
1 is added to 2 to make 3
4 is added to 5 to make 6
but similar symbols disappear if added together.

20

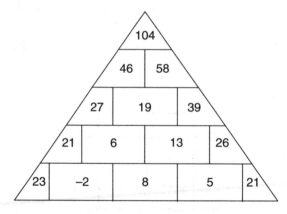

Assessment

19 – 20 Exceptional
16 – 18 Excellent
13 – 15 Very good
10 – 12 Good
 6 – 9   Average

IQ test three

1   E; dots are turning from black to white in turn, first one
     in the vertical column then one in the horizontal line.

2   136
     $9 + 4 = 13, 2 \times 3 = 6$. Similarly $8 + 2 = 10, 3 \times 4 = 12$.

3   B; the figures change places as in the original analogy
     i.e. first to second, second to fourth, third to first,
     fourth to third.

4   C; looking at alternate squares across and down, circles
     and squares are added in turn.

5   147
     The numbers 47231 are being repeated in the same
     order.

6

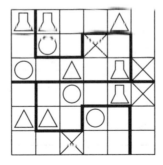

7   C; only lines appearing just once in either of the first
     two squares are carried forward to the third square
     looking across and down.

8   C

9   5

Look at diagonal lines from bottom right-hand corner to top. The bottom and third digits multiplied together produce the number formed by the second and top digits. So $5 \times 7 = 35$. Similarly $3 \times 8 = 24$, $9 \times 4 = 36$ and $7 \times 6 = 42$.

10   A; every fourth figure has a black circle at the top, every fifth figure has a white circle in the middle and every second figure has a white circle with a dot at the bottom.

11   C
$3^2 + 4^2 + 5^2 + 6^2 + 64 - 56 = 94$

12   Pineapple   24p
     Ugli fruit   7p

13   A

14   11

7	9	4
10	6	4
10	9	1
5	6	9
2	17	1
2	11	7
6	6	8
7	6	7
5	8	7
5	11	4
2	9	9

15   91
     $47 + 35$ (53 reversed) = 82
     $73 + 18$ (18 reversed) = 91

16   A = 5
      B = 2
      C = 7
      D = 1
      E = 4
      F = 3
      G = 8
      H = 6

17   2

$$\frac{\cancel{17}}{\cancel{23}} \times \frac{\cancel{46}^{\,2}}{8} \times \frac{\cancel{16}^{\,2}}{\cancel{34}_{\,2}}$$

18   45

18	10
26	13
29	17
16	7
19	16
108	− 63

19   14¾
      There are two series: −1¾ and + 1½

20   47
      $(7 \times 4) + 19 = 47$

Assessment

19 – 20 Exceptional
16 – 18 Excellent
13 – 15 Very good
10 – 12 Good
 6 – 9   Average

IQ test four

1 F

2 D; so that each horizontal and vertical line contains seven black and seven white dots.

3 D; the large arc moves 180°, the next largest moves 90° anti-clockwise and the smallest arc moves 90° clockwise.

4 3   3
   6   8

   Start at the bottom left corner and repeat the numbers 38496 working up the first column and down the second, etc.

5 C; A and G are the same; as are D and F, B and H, and I and E.

6 A; the circles move round one place clockwise at each stage; however, the dot previously at the top left-hand corner always changes black to white or vice-versa at the next stage.

7 ●

8 3

9 D; the first, third and fifth components turn round.

10 D

11 C; swirl moves 120° clockwise; black dot moves corner to corner of the pentagon clockwise; pentagon moves 60° clockwise.

12 D

13

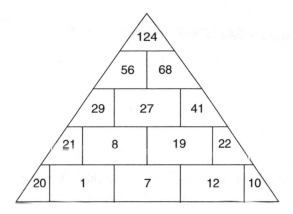

14   F
     F = 15⁷⁄₈   The rest = 15⁵⁄₈

15   28

16   218
     11 × 7 =   77   13 × 11 = 143   27 × 8 = 216
     17 × 9 = 153   17 × 11 = 187   31 × 14 = 434
difference   76   44   218

17   Edward

18   G
     A and D are the same, as are B and E, and C and F.

19   225 + 119 + 76 + 80 = 500

20   A scored 100; B scored 16; C scored 41; D scored 12
     and E scored 31.

Assessment

19 – 20 Exceptional
16 – 18 Excellent
13 – 15 Very good
10 – 12 Good
 6 – 9   Average

IQ test five

1   D; so that the dot is within the intersection of three curved lines.

2   E; each circle in the top section is repeated in the bottom section, but rotated 90° anti-clockwise.

3   24
    One man builds 2/3 of a wall in a day. Therefore, six men would build 12/3 = 4 walls a day, or 24 walls in 6 days.

4   D; looking across and down, the contents of the final square are determined by the contents of the first two squares. Lines from the first two squares are carried forward to the third, but when two lines appear in the same position in these two squares they are cancelled out.

5   8

6   3   1   5   2   6   4   (or reverse)

7   B; individual components turn over and change from black/white or vice versa as in the original analogy.

8   E; the large square is disappearing a side at each stage working clockwise and the small square is being constructed a side at a time working anti-clockwise.

9   48 socks
    If he took out 46 socks they could all be the blue and red socks. To make sure he also has a pair of black socks he must take out two more.

10 B; the three blocks are rearranged in the same order as in the original analogy and all become upright i.e. far left goes to right, far right goes bottom left and middle goes top left.

11   C

12   729; each number is doubled and then 7 is added to make the next.

13   $1\frac{3}{4}$

14   A

$$\frac{18}{9} \times \frac{330}{8} = 82\frac{1}{2}$$

15   F = 513

16   109; add the two digits together for each number, and add onto that number to produce the next number.
56   67   89   88   104   109
    +11   +13   +8   +16   +5

17   85 (+ 10, −5)

18
◯ 10   • 1   △ 7   ● 4

19   E
1 is added to 2 to equal 3
4 is added to 5 to equal 6
but similar symbols disappear when added together.

20   2C

Assessment

19 – 20   Exceptional
16 – 18   Excellent
13 – 15   Very good
10 – 12   Good
  6 – 9   Average

IQ test six

1   A

2   C; at each stage working from left to right a line becomes vertical. It then alternates horizontal/vertical at each stage. The first line always remains horizontal.

3   A; each symbol changes to another symbol as in the original analogy. Black symbols always change to white and vice versa. So, for example, in the first analogy a white oval becomes a black star, therefore in the second analogy a white star becomes a black oval.

4   Tuesday

5   B; the contents of each pentagon are determined by the contents of the two pentagons immediately below it. When lines are common to these pentagons they are not carried forward to the pentagon above.

6   BCD

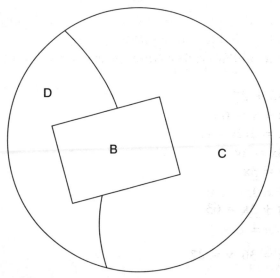

7   3
    6 + 3 = 9, 9/3 = 3.
    Similarly 7 + 5 = 12, 12/3 = 4 and 9 + 6 = 15, 15/3 = 5

8   A; the straight line becomes curved, the circle at the end
    of the line changes from black to white, the black dot
    becomes a white star and the white oval becomes a black
    dot, thus completing the metamorphosis.

9   7; the middle row totals 15, the fourth and sixth rows
    total 13, the third and seventh rows total 11, the second
    and eighth rows total 9, therefore the top and bottom
    rows should be 7.

10 B; start at the top left-hand corner and work along the
    top row and back along the second row, etc. repeating
    the four different arrangements of circles. Thus the
    bottom row is the reverse of the top row, and the third
    row is the reverse of the second row.

11 C
    1 is added to 2 to equal 3
    4 is added to 5 to equal 6
    but similar symbols disappear when added together.

12 36 + 27
    $x + y = 63$
    $x = 2(2y - x)$
    $3x = 4y$
    $y = \dfrac{3x}{4}$
    $x + \dfrac{3x}{4} = 63$
    $x = 36, y = 27$

13   8
A $(6 + 15 + 19) - (7 + 11 + 10) = 12$
B $(17 + 19 + 2) - (14 + 16 + 2) = 6$
C $(11 + 7 + 5) - (3 + 8 + 2) = 10$

14   102
Octagon sides $8 \times 17 = 136$
Hexagon sides $6 \times 17 = 102$
Pentagon sides $5 \times 17 = 85$
Square sides $4 \times 17 = 68$
Triangle sides $3 \times 17 = 51$

15   190
Find factors and multiply them together
$37 = 37 \times \cancel{1}$
$19 = 19 \times \cancel{1}$ $\dfrac{7030}{37} = 190$
$10 = 5 \times 2$
$5 = 5 \times \cancel{1}$

16   12
267
276
279
297 (turn 6 upside down)
627
672
726
729
762
792
927
972

17   D
      1 is added to 2 to equal 3
      4 is added to 5 to equal 6
      but similar symbols disappear when added together.

18   16
      Numbers are primes, reversed
      31 – 37 – 41 – 43 – 47 – 53 – 59 – 61

19   C
      1 is added to 2 to equal 3
      4 is added to 5 to equal 6
      but similar symbols disappear when added together.

20   2C

Assessment

19 – 20 Exceptional
16 – 18 Excellent
13 – 15 Very good
10 – 12 Good
 6 – 9   Average

IQ test seven

1   E; each line and column contains one of the three
    different symbols. In each line of columns just one
    symbol appears black and just one symbol appears
    upside-down.

2   15

3   A; the circle becomes an ellipse, the square becomes a
    trapezium and the diamond becomes a triangle.

4   2; each ring contains the numbers 1 to 9 once each
    only.

5

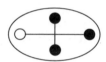

Lines and dots are added until the cross is formed and
dots change black to white and vice versa at each stage.

6   E

7   1
    $7 \times 3 = 21$. Similarly $7 \times 5 = 35$, $6 \times 8 = 48$
    and $2 \times 9 = 18$

8   A; looking across and down the line moves 45°
    clockwise, the black dot moves 90° clockwise and the
    white dot moves 90° anti-clockwise.

9 D; as in the original analogy, the rectangle at the top moves to the bottom, the one in the middle moves to the top and the one at the bottom moves to the middle. The symbol at the top moves to the middle, the symbol in the middle moves to the bottom and the symbol at the bottom moves to the top.

10 352 (32 × 11)

11 A;

$\diagup$ moves one corner clockwise

◯ moves one corner clockwise

● moves one side anti-clockwise

⊙ moves to opposite corner

○ moves half a side anti-clockwise

• moves one corner clockwise

12 43 (7 × 9) − (5 × 4)

13 5

$$\frac{26 + 3 + 7 + 6 + 8}{10}$$

14 81 ÷ 9 × 17 + 6 − 59 = 100

15 3
    There are two series: − 3¼ and + 2¾

16   624

6	12	19	27	30	35	38	41	89
7	13	20	28	31	36	39	42	90
		21						

17   20
First column in A + first column in B = 35
Second column in A + second column in B = 36
Third column in A + third column in B = 37
Fourth column in A + fourth column in B = 38
Fifth column in A + fifth column in B = 39

18    $30\frac{1}{2}$; add $6\frac{3}{4}$

19   C

20   A
1 is added to 2 to equal 3
4 is added to 5 to equal 6
but similar symbols disappear when added together.

Assessment

19 – 20   Exceptional
16 – 18   Excellent
13 – 15   Very good
10 – 12   Good
 6 – 9   Average